THE LOG OF THE
SKIPPER'S WIFE

THE LOG OF THE SKIPPER'S *WIFE*

James W. Balano

Down East Books
Camden, Maine

Copyright © 1979 by James W. Balano

ISBN 0-089272-062-X

Library of Congress Catalog Card Number 79-52446

Printer at Versa Press, East Peoria, IL

12   14   15   13

DOWN EAST BOOKS
Camden, Maine

For Book Orders Call: (800) 685-7962
www.downeastbooks.com

To Elsie Gage Balano, my wife,
who quelled several family mutinies,
which allowed me to piece this work together.

PREFACE

THE FIRST THING that comes to mind for a preface to my mother's diary is that she always got a big kick out of the fact that her sea-going husband had no time for learning how to spell the word "preface." Captain Fred got the letters right by taking the first of each of the following words: Peter Rabbit Eats Fish And Catches Eels. As long as he could use words relating to the sea, he could remember how to spell. Thus, with her help Schenectady was composed of the abbreviation for the word schooner, Sch, followed by his familiar ENE, for east-northeast. That got him as far as Schene, and from there on she told him he was on his own and that if he couldn't remember the "ctady" he should call her. He persevered and came up with the congenial thought that Cod Tongues Are Dandy. For him, this was extremely satisfying inefficiency, but it was never to be forgotten by me; I still use it. And cod tongues *are* dandy!

When my mother told of her Sioux Indian neighbors in Yellow Medicine County, Minnesota, where she was born on November 25, 1882, Captain Fred felt uneasy because there were no conceivable sea words for use in memorizing the spelling of the word Sioux. I believe he went to his grave with that one unsolved. It helped a bit when she told him it was a French way to spell Su but she got way past him when she opined that Su, in turn, was the Altaic word for water. Now water rang a bell with him, and for years to come he would tell friends that his wife had known some water Indians who, of course, must have been all right, being sailors.

So good at words was Dorothea Honora Moulton Balano that she learned enough Sioux to converse with a band of Dakota Sioux who visited her father's quarter-section farm to bid her father farewell as they embarked on their long trek to sanctuary in Canada. The Sioux presented my mother and her two sisters and brother with homemade dolls. She was four years old, and saying good-bye to the "washtay" (good) Indian neighbors, she said, made her feel terribly "seechidough" (bad). My mother told me that her diary started then, but that part of it has never been found. To make up for the loss, she later had her mother and her grandmother write down their impressions of those days and add some history of the family. Those old notebooks are filled with the westward trend of Moultons, Putnams, Kennedys, Brewsters, and Dorrances from Plymouth and Salem to Maine, Vermont, New York State, Illinois, Minnesota and beyond.

Those notebooks tell how Dorothea's grandmother Martin held a looking glass to the mouth of her daughter Laura Martin Dorrance to determine whether there was any breath left in the baby during a bout with pneumonia in the blizzard of 1850. The nearest doctor was two hundred miles across the prairie. Of more concern to the women was the absence of a minister. All through the faded pages of the copybooks are hopes that their little congregation might entice a man of God to join them. They needed someone who could dwell on the Word Sundays and on Work the rest of the week; they could not pay him for ministering, but they might feed him and provide shelter.

Dorothea learned from the itinerant ministers and from her mother. She devoured the Blackstone of her Justice of the Peace father. At nine she was sent to the local school at the County Seat and went home to help with spring planting, summer cultivating, and the harvest. After high school she had to teach for two years to earn enough money for train tickets to Minneapolis and the University of Minnesota, where, fortunately, she had a fairly well-to-do relative, Aunt Sue Kingman, who helped out with room, board, friends of cultural interest, and, most important, an introduction to opportunity for indulging Dorothea's in-born taste for travel. Aunt Sue was a Brewster. She thought more of her electric car, than of being a Mayflower descendant.

And travel Dora did. Her summer vacation trips to the Pacific and to Canada were exuberantly noted in her diary of 1908-09, as was her decision to get away from mere U.S. and Canadian travel by signing up to teach in Puerto Rico.

The diary as I know it was started in 1908 in cheap notebooks. She told me several times that she would one day edit it for publication. The author, Peter B. Kyne, one of whose books was *Cappy Ricks*, the story of Matt Peaseley of Thomaston, Maine, once got her to help him in sea-going terminology. Upon learning that she had kept a diary, he offered to help her ready it for publishing. At the time they were working on his book in San Francisco during a short visit there by Dorothea and her husband when he was master of the steamer *Peter Crowell*. But the World War interfered, and Dorothea immersed herself in war activities, building the Port Clyde Public Library, promoting chapters of the Daughters of the American Revolution, journeying to distant ports to meet her husband, then a commander in charge of transports to France, running the local Port Clyde estate of her husband, and, between six and seven each evening, inundating my brother and me with books written in three languages.

After World War I, Dorothea went to sea with Captain Fred in steam, visiting much of Europe, North Africa, South America, and the West Indies, none of which was covered by diary but most of which was related to me by letter and conversation. From 1923 to 1927, she lived at Gardena, California, in order to be near the ports of Wilmington and San Pedro to which her husband's ship came north from the Panama Canal en route from Liverpool, Glasgow, Hamburg, and Antwerp. She made several of those trips with him and went along the Pacific Coast as well with him. Then she "went ashore," because Captain Fred took a shore job in New York as a marine insurance executive. Although the family got to Maine several times a year and continued to feel that New York was no more than a port of call, Dorothea saw and heard every opera at the Metropolitan several times each, became Regent of the State

D.A.R., more or less ran the National Motion Picture Board of Review in order to see more movies than she thought she ought to pay to see, and, each September, deloused my clothes when I would come home from a summer trip at sea, starting at age thirteen, wages twenty-seven dollars a month.

So Dorothea had little time for editing what she called "my scribbling" and less interest in the past than in her hectic present, and her plans for future trips to "just anywhere." She took my brother and me to do the Grand Tour of Europe one summer, when I would have preferred to accept the glorious job of bosun, which was offered me at the age of sixteen by a Maine skipper. My brother and I spent the two months visiting cathedrals, with one eye on the lookout for Coca Cola signs. She made us drink our first beer in Lucerne, because we had entered the beerhall where Wagner composed parts of the Ring, drinking beer. She was indomitable, and her spirit comes through a bit in the *Log of the Skipper's Wife*.

Maine skippers often took their wives to sea, as did other seafarers. Europeans still do it. In my parents' day, many master mariners owned part of their ships, and most of them felt as though they owned the whole ship. There was no question of insurance or Coast Guard regulations. Going to sea with your wife was the accepted thing. As late as 1927 my mother went to sea with her husband, and she took along a sister who became engaged to the chief engineer. Whole families, such as the Colcord family of Searsport, lived aboard ship. Lincoln and Johanna Colcord looked upon their father's square rigger as their home, their school, and their asylum from provincial boredom. For anyone thinking it unusual that a family prefer a home at sea to one ashore, I recommend a trip to Hong Kong where many families still live afloat. Short of that, join Dorothea for a voyage down to the sea "in a tall ship with a star to steer her by."

James Wilfred Balano
BUCKSPORT, MAINE

THE LOG OF THE
SKIPPER'S WIFE

JUNE 21, 1910, (Utuado, Puerto Rico)

Hell of a day! Exams for my eighth graders but no mail from the States. The *SS Carolina* spitefully had a collision in New York Harbor, and her mail bags are rumored to be sent on the *SS Caracas* for arrival next week. Ojala. [Editor's note: *Ojala* is a word that comes from the Moslem occupation of Spain and is a plea to Allah.]

As Betty and I were booked on the *Carolina* for our return trip to New York after two years' exile, we'll be desperate to find another way of getting home. Betty's beau, a Captain Balano from Maine, has often schemed to take her north, with me as chaperone. Chaperone? Bah!

Think of something more pleasant than being a chaperone, a kill-joy, an envious witness to rounds of tickle and slap. Oh, yes! Had the time of my life Saturday night. Good Latin music. I do love flutes in a dance orchestra. How these latinos can fandango! They loved my yellow dress. Drank champagne and mercy it's expensive stuff. Don Jorge's inherited thousands will soon evaporate at the rate we downed the bubbly.

1

JUNE 23, 1910

I wonder if we shall sail north on Captain Balano's schooner. Also hope! No! I'll bet it's ridden with fleas and cockroaches. He once kidded Betty, telling her cockroaches on board were good signs; hungry ships don't attract roaches, he said. But if his four-master is half as clean and nice as the *Governor Powers,* which Betty and I visited to see Captain and Mrs. Kent of Cutler, Maine, it'll be heavenly. The *Powers* is a Maine vessel, too.

JUNE 25, 1910

First came a letter from Betty Holbrook with a photo of her captain. A wonderful Roman nose and eyes to match, roaming. I wonder! Then a telegram from Betty saying we're invited to sail north with him. I felt like refusing out of plain contrariness. To be a chaperone of that man? After having chaperoned my eighth grade all year! But, being contrary, I got contrary against my contrariness and sent word I'd go. What convulsions of reasoning can be prompted by the picture of a good-looking young sea captain. Poor Betty! God bless her and help her. I'll take a load of magazines and books along to keep me and my eyes busy. I don't want to take them at all.

JUNE 29, 1910

On board the schooner *R.W. Hopkins* at Aguirre Sugar Central, Puerto Rico. So much has happened this past four days I can hardly write about it adequately. First Betty's telegram; then going to Ponce. Ferns on the mountain rocks, immense, stately clouds hanging on the mountain peaks we passed by, last view of the mists in the hills as we descended to the southern coastal plain. The clouds and mists hanging on to lovely Puerto Rico until the trade winds pushed them west. And that exquisite nineteenth-kilometer stop for sliced pineapple and chunks of papaya in the little hacienda guest house overlooking the blue Caribbean from up high on the mountain divide. No refund check from the steamship company, but that didn't ruin the trip, not much. Captain Balano is not only handsome with a smile that melts but also seems perfectly splendid, as well. Betty is a lucky girl and a perfect darling.

Friday morning, JULY 1, 1910, (Aguirre)

Dinner Wednesday night on board the *Governor Powers* with Betty, Captain Balano, and the Kents. Aren't they the loveliest people. Have been so busy I've slighted you, my diary, so now to calmly retrace the progress. At Ponce, Betty and I engaged two coaches to come along the coast to Aguirre. One contained the trunks and the other Betty and yours truly. Some auto drivers offered to take us, but we scornfully turned them away and had eyes only for the horses and the *coches* with white fringed tops. Without noise and bumping we could chat like civilized people. Betty is afraid she'll be seasick. I hope she won't be. Don't feel like being a nurse as well as chaperone.

Arrived at Aguirre, and Betty bravely sailed into the office of the sugar company to ask for Captain Balano. I don't believe those poor lads have yet recovered from their surprise. They passed us through the gates and down to the wharf. We walked and talked and consulted and finally sat ourselves dignifiedly down and quietly waited in our coach. I hailed some boys, and they assured me with all the duplicity of which they are masters that they would walk the narrow brow to the schooner and get the Captain. Young ladies aren't supposed to range the Puerto Rican waterfront soliciting seamen. They went with knowing smiles, but soon our Captain appeared. Such a lovely schooner, four masts. She must be a beauty when the sails are up. A charmingly arranged little cabin. We have the Captain's room. Two is company and. . . what was I going to say?

Sunday morning, JULY 3, 1910

Thursday evening came Marco, the general factotum from the sugar central, he of the "yes, yes, yes," which he apparently uses all the

time whether he means it or not. With him were two young
heathens from the mill — chemists they were, out to see what prizes
the Captain had got. In Spanish the word is *procurado*, procured.
They came and saw but did not conquer. One was a quiet, little lad
from Hawaii, with enormous, unquiet eyes.

And Friday — such a day! We went on shore in the morning to
call on the Merhofs, the doctor whose little Puerto Rican wife is a
cousin of the Utuado·Caballeros. Saw the McClains and Miss Wood
in a beautiful large home on top of the hill where flamboyan trees
were gloriously red. The house has about a million rooms, with a
schoolroom on the third floor overlooking miles upon miles of
shimmering gray-blue sea hedged by broken lines of foam and surf
and islands that invite. As luck would have it, Dame Fortune smiled
on us, or was it Captain Balano who smiled, and we went for a drive
along the beautiful coast to Guayama in the McClains' auto.
Returned to Merhof's for a lunch of succulent *lechon asado*, roast
young piglets on spits with sauces. Paris could envy. There we met
Mrs. Chisholm. Curiosity killed a cat but never a Chisholm!

Saturday came a letter from the steamship company agreeing to
refund our passage money on the *Carolina*, but no check, of course.
Betty and I went with the Captain to the Customs Office at Arroyo to
clear for Boston. The man with the three "yesses" accompanied us,
but Captain Balano did the work. More smiles from Dame Fortune?
Returning, that villainous *cochero* wanted to bring a goat along in a
box, but Betty and I could not agree to suffer his blatting all the way
back to the ship, so finally the creature was removed, with much
blatting from the goat and the *cochero*. We returned in peace and
smelled the sea instead of the animal. Just as bad was being
intercepted by Mrs. Chisholm as we neared the wharf. She wanted
us for lunch, she said, but we knew it was to feed the rumor mill, so
we pleaded headaches.

When we arrived on board, the awning was down as the crew
prepared the ship for an early sailing in the morning. I got sea fever
and couldn't think of sleeping. Such a night! Even the little stars
were out, and there was a small new moon on the horizon. Wrote
letters for the States mail, telling my poor family of the venture
their wayward daughter is undertaking.

All sails set and we look like a great, white, winged bird as we roll stately over a sapphire sea along a dim outline of hazy mountains. It was a memorable experience to wake from a short nap at four in the morning to the sound of creaking rigging. Barely did we rush into a few clothes and scurry on deck when the mizzen sail majestically lifted and straightened. The gray darkness slowly lightened, and we watched the fore and main sails rise against the little, low moon. Halyards loosened and slackened, finally taking their proper lengths. Great booms swung into position with the breeze. With the coming of dawn and a great ball of sun, Captain Balano whistled for the pilot to hurry aboard. He spoke only the King's Spanish, and I was happy to translate a bit, although I found that seaman's talk is neither English nor Spanish but a code of grunts, pointing, and gesticulation.

To avoid the mud shoals in the narrow channel and lift the ship on her way, the spanker had to be partly hoisted for a few minutes. That extra power did the work and soon we were free, the prow, *proa*, pointing west. With a lazy majesty and billowing grace, the good ship *R.W. Hopkins* put to sea as though some stately creature had communed with the moon and stars and then bowed to their master, the sun, who would now lead the way.

She is loaded with molasses, a cargo valued at fourteen thousand dollars. Shall I write my W.C.T.U. mother that New England rum will be the end product? No! I'll concentrate on the use of molasses for cookies.

Out through the buoys, black on the starboard bow and red on the port, the pilot said *adios*. He had made thirty-nine dollars, paid by the Central, and an easy gain because the Captain piloted the pilot.

A man is always at the wheel. The mate eats at our table; the second mate and the engineer eat at the second table. I ate a hearty breakfast, but poor Betty did not. I don't know how much more I can eat without letting out a few seams. And I'm ashamed to be seen enjoying food so much in front of Betty. She told the Captain that her stomach was weak, and he didn't help matters at all by telling her she must have a strong stomach by the way she was throwing food over the side farther than anyone he had ever seen. The brute!

Eight bells is either four, eight, or twelve o'clock. Each half hour is marked by lovely bells.

After the buoys and the pilot became ancient history, the crew hoisted the jibs, outer, flying, main, and forestay-sail, and finished raising the largest sail on board, the spanker. Then the topsails were loosened and set, all four. We plowed past Caja de Muertos at eight when the watch was changed. Betty still seasick and the Captain scrubbing the dirt of land off his white paint. I'd take a bath but am sure this sea would toss me out of the tub. The wind is dead aft and breezing up. I'll tell my farmer-father that it comes from the rear. I hope that if I do get sick it won't be until Betty is better. The Captain asked me to help him stand the evening watch on deck. He seems every inch a man, and a handsome one at that. I wonder; I wonder how it will all come out. *Dios sabe.*

JULY 5, 1910

Betty is better today.

JULY 6, 1910

Dorothea Moulton, you are the biggest fool that ever lived! I am heartily ashamed of you. Am too disgusted with you to write any more. You should have told him in a nice way that you were ticklish or something, instead of enjoying it. Poor, dear Betty. Please hurry up and get well.

JULY 7, 1910

A flying fish flew on board this morning and died soon after striking the deck. Royal purple and soft opalescent sunset last night as seen from my deck chair atop the house, or is it called the after cabin? Betty is a little better. My saltwater bath with saltwater soap is awaiting. I'll soak and think. Does that lovely copper bathtub give off thoughts?

Today is our fifth day out and the good breeze holds. The *R.W.H.* slides along easily over the swells. Such sapphire water up forward under the bow. I sat there for hours yesterday, still thinking, among the anchors, jibs, bowsprit, and jibboom. Iron chains by the dozens, and the capstan painted a hideous pink so it can be seen at night.

The life of a common sailor is worse than that of a slave. This Captain sells them clothes and soap and tobacco at one hundred percent or more profit to be paid for from their paltry twenty-five dollars a month wage. Perfectly scandalous! Remember that, my girl, when next he casts those roaming eyes on you and smiles. Ship's philosophy: keep them in debt so they can't afford to leave, especially a good cook. Sailors are sometimes put in chains in the lazarette. Went below to see it yesterday and rummaged through my trunk to find my tennis shoes. Now I can move about with greater assurance against the rolls and pitches. But instead of more exploring must write some letters. Still owe part of my college tuition loan, must also write parents who'd never believe all of this way out on the Minnesota farm.

The Captain cornered me for sunset coffee and stayed on deck with me talking about his home at Port Clyde, Maine. Was he trying to woo? I've nothing to say about what followed. Nothing to say, my daughter. Guess I'll spend these heavenly days on top of the after deckhouse where the view is mutually good: I can see the beautiful sea and everyone else can see what goes on between the two deck chairs. I do wish Betty would get well. It's I, now, who needs the chaperone.

Saw by the chart that we're nearly halfway to Boston. I wonder if my *Carolina* refund will be awaiting me.

When the Captain asks me about my plans, I get him to teach me seamanship. The gaffs are the upper booms on the larger sails. Dog watches from four to six and six to eight are stood in order to change the watches so that the two watches will rotate each day. All this is not only interesting but also gets his nibs and me through the long tea or coffee on top of the after deckhouse.

Friday, JULY 8, 1910. (Latitude: 30 North; Longitude: 68 West)

Passed the SS *Ponce* bound for Puerto Rico from New York. She whistled to us, and we saluted by dipping the ensign. How's that for success in my seamanship classes?

But less success in my latest romance. What liars these sea captains are. Each day I change my mind about him.

Sunday, JULY 10, 1910

At sea a week today. Almost becalmed this morning as the trade winds played out. Had early morning coffee with the Captain. Isn't that doing well for one who started to detest him. But there's no doubt he's all man and, after Don Jorge and his ilk, that's something.

A rent was torn in the spanker sail last night, and at three bells, or one thirty in the morning, I went on deck to see it lowered. Now the men are mending it atop the deckhouse, and I have no place to sit so I'll take a promenade along forward over the deck cargo and watch the dolphins race us. They're delightful and apparently talk to each other with delightful squeals.

Becalmed and the booms creak and shake about the masts for want of wind. How I do enjoy my saltwater plunge every morning. Got Betty to take one, and it spruced her up so that she's finally made it up to the deck chairs where the Captain is jollying her. The poor darling can stand a lot of it. Superstitious Captain threw an old pair of shoes into the sea to bring wind. Shades of Ulysses!

JULY 12, 1910

Wind changed to the west. Tacking ship.

"All hands on deck. Ease off your brail lines. Let fore, main, and mizzen come over. Over with your jibs. Loosen the spanker tackle. That's well. Now let her go port a half point more. Steer no'th no'th-east."

Spanker sail down again today for more repairs. Hoisted a new foretopsail. Putting on stronger sails for the strong westerlies. I took pictures up forward today and got Betty to do so, also. A glorious sunset and the *Hopkins* family, or should I say *menage a trois*, stayed on deck to watch the moon sink into the sea like the disappearance of a pink-and-rose seashell. Betty was tired and went below. I can only say, as a result of her leaving and my staying: "Whom the Gods destroy they first make mad." And try to remember that, my dear.

JULY 13, 1910

"Let go the spanker sheet and haul out on the boom tackles. Let go the jib sheets and let the jibs go over the stays."

Captain stopped the clock today while tacking so that the man at the wheel could stay a half hour longer so as not to take a man from handling the sails. When the poor fellow complained, the Captain scolded him for sleeping at the wheel. The detestable lack of logic!

On deck all day enjoying the change from tropical weather to the billowing blue-gray of northern seas. The sun shamefacedly peering from behind dismal clouds and the air cool enough for sweaters.

JUNE 14, er, JULY 14, 1910

That villainous Captain has me all mixed up.

A school of whales this morning. Also a huge three-masted squarerigger bound out for wonderful Europe. Maybe I'll yet get there. That's one consideration in any decision about marrying a seagoing man. She was a beautiful ship; a Norwegian, says the skipper.

JULY 15, 1910

A squall last night. I was sleepy with all the fresh air and retired early. Was it premonition? The Captain and Betty stayed on deck. He broke the news to her. I wonder, I wonder! He woke me before dawn and looked so huge and reliable in his old black sou'wester and oilskins. The sea was phosphorescent, and the good schooner cut through the lighted billows with a zip. Captain told me I must be feeling at home if I could sleep through such a rushing squall with which he had to contend most of the night. It tore away the main topsail, and now we have a headwind out of the northwest, which retards our progress materially. Will it be Boston on Sunday? And will my little one hundred be there? I wonder.

Sunday, JULY 17, 1910

It is not Boston, but a good northeaster is blowing us along wonderfully. Still something like one hundred miles to go. No sun for sights.

Tuesday, JULY 19,1910

Still at sea. Going north in some channel or other to get around Cape Cod. Reached Nantucket light Sunday evening, and I've been freezing ever since. Bad weather: no sun, no wind, tide rips, choppy sea. Bah! And I don't know what the Captain and Betty are up to now. I see where yours truly, to preserve her peace of mind, will have to cultivate the embroidery habit and the solitaire habit on this schooner. These sea captains!

A school of mackerel yesterday and one of cod today. Many two-masted fishing schooners around us. Passed Cape Cod Light. Some steamers bound for Europe and several large sailing ships. The seamen are scraping the bitts, preparing to varnish them for docking.

JULY 30, 1910

En route for home and Mama. Arrived in Boston Friday, a long week ago and, oh! wasn't it good to see the States. On deck early in the morning to greet the towboat and Boston harbor with its forts, a revenue cutter, and steamers from Maine and New York. Houses with strangely peaked roofs to shed the snows I'd nearly forgotten. Houses with more windows and short green grass lawns, unlike the luxurious vegetation of the tropics. But being in the States again and Boston at that! And I got my check from the ship chandlers. Nearly all of it went to pay for excess baggage for my trunks to get to Minnesota.

Boston is a dear old town. And we had such a dinner! Never will I forget that first dinner in the States for over two years. Such steak, such salad, and such apple pie a la mode! The intellectual waitress who served us was amazed at my calling the repast ambrosia and nectar of the Gods. Boston-like, she said it was material stuff with which to nourish our coy oral entities.

Then to Captain Balano's home at Port Clyde, Maine. A long drive in his father's Regal auto to Boothbay, where we took a little mailboat to Monhegan and Port Clyde, a beautiful spot of granite rocks, evergreens, and much saltwater. Fred's home is too dear for words, and I knew it at once from the pictures. Met Captain Archibald, who owns a fleet of coastal steamers. He told me, while Fred was somewhere exploring the boat, that Fred always brought home nice new girls. I replied that during the trip north I had counted over forty-one of them, from his lies, and then got tired.

Monhegan's cliffs impressed me more than the forty-one girls, as did the lighthouse and the blueberry pie we had on Sunday. Visited his grandmother in the woods, and she asked, "Be you from here or be you from away?"! Pure Devon dialect, although her ancestors have been here since the beginnings. She used to go by sloop to meet her seagoing husband at Salem. On Monday Fred drove me to Rockland, and then on to Boston, that night. He sails a ship much better than an auto. I don't know how, but we made it. He tacked and beat to windward most of the way, much to the consternation of several drivers of horses and oxen.

That lovely Mrs. Hopkins took me all over Boston, the Common, and the Frog Pond where the British soldiers placed ashes to ruin the boys' skating; the toboggan run, where General Gates made his soldiers let the boys slide. Saw the Shaw monument and the flags in Memorial Hall at the State House. Something for a descendant of the *Mayflower* Brewsters and Bradfords to conjure with. I must remember to tell Mama, who tried to tell me of these things without ever having seen them herself. I must be more attentive to my heritage. Saw the tattered emblems of a hundred Massachusetts regiments commemorating the noble work of a half-dozen wars, the codfish of the Gloucester men, Fred's ancestors. There is a safe which holds the *Mayflower's* log brought from England after twenty years' negotiations by Senator Hoar. Saw his tomb at Concord in the Sleepy Hollow cemetery. It has a grand epitaph: "I do not believe in destiny or blind force. I believe in the living God and the American people. I believe that today is better than yesterday and that tomorrow will be better than today." After the past two years fraught with Latin fatalism, that is refreshing. As Fred said during the trip: "I make my own luck!"

Hawthorne's grave contains a small headpiece about as large as this page (Editor's note: The diary page is 6″ x 8″.); Emerson's is a rough stone with a small bronze tablet and by his side is his wife's, topped by a bas relief of tulips, a beautiful thing. Alcott's and Thoreau's are plain, large stones, Concord-style, the style which I now see was carried west by such pioneers as my grandparents, who set up little Concords all through the country.

Mrs. Hopkins told me that the bones of the British soldiers, buried near the Common, had been dug up when the subway was laid. Am I growing a bunion?

Fred and I lunched at Marsten's with Alice Hatch and her husband. Such chicken pie, um! Never will I forget Boston cooking or that delicious chocolate pie in Portland.

In the afternoon to the Public Library. More bunions. Saw French's lions, Sargent's law and prophets, the frieze of the holy grail recalling the opera Parsifal. There is a newspaper room containing papers in many languages: Greek, Spanish, French, Jewish, and, I suppose, North Polar. At the art museum there was a good LeRolle, some Romneys, not to mention a Buddha, whom I saluted in true Catholic, Puerto Rican style. Not so many pictures as New York, but wonderful. Boston needs some Goulds and Vanderbilts to purchase more old treasures for her. New Englanders don't part from their money too easily, as I noticed at Port Clyde when Fred's mother paid off an errand boy with a half-rotten apple.

At Bliss's, the ship chandler, got a note from Betty, wishing me all happiness. She said she was writing the story of her life. I can't take the time to do that.

Had a supper of raspberries at the Hatches, and how Fred did eat. Somehow got Fred to the theatre twice. He was so bored that each time he went out to talk to the policeman on the corner at intermission and did not return. Do I civilize him or is it hopeless? I wonder about this future of ours together. Perhaps Betty would be better for him after all. She doesn't get bunions or do too much exploring or get enchanted with plays, opera, and books.

Changed reservations so as to have a last evening with Fred and his friends on the schooner. He begged me to, saying he wanted to impress somebody with the fact that an old salt like him could land a girl who'd been to college and knew the difference between the sharp and dull ends of a ship. Caught the late train for Buffalo by one minute, after saying good-bye to both Captain Crowell and Mr. Thurlow, shipowners, who have part of Fred's vessel as well as many others. Fred gave me a picture of the *Hopkins* as a going-away present. Am I ever going to see her again? Still wondering, knowing him.

Saw Niagara but was moved to profanity I'd learned from Fred at the site of the tough and uncouth crowds. Betty would have said there's a difference between a gloved and veiled crowd, and one ungloved and unveiled.

Oh, my boy, my handsome boy. Why do people ever have to part? And here begins a new chapter of my log. Let us hope it will have as much of good fortune and the good Lord's blessing as this one has.

JULY 31, 1910

On board steamer *Northwest* bound for Duluth. How she shakes and smokes. It should not be afforded the seaman's loving "she" but should be called "it." The thing shakes and smokes, not at all like a beautiful sailing ship. Fred would be disgusted. Shall I ever see my Fred again? I wonder, I wonder. And *si dios quiere* I shall soon know of his sincerity. God grant that he does as he promised, and we will have years together of happiness. If he means what he said all will be well, even with hard knocks now and then.

MAY 14, 1911

Aguirre, Puerto Rico, on board the *Hopkins*.

How I hate to keep a diary! That's evident from the date of the preceding entry. Nearly a year has passed. Meanwhile, a few things happened.

We were married, believe it or not. It was a private but beautiful ceremony conducted at the home of Fred's cousin, Alice Balano Davidson, in Melrose, Massachusetts. Her husband, Herbert, a great musician who sells hams, sang for us the appropriate tunes. Fred, typically, arrived late, having been spending the day hunting for my mislaid trunk, which contained my self-made trousseau. He also was scouring the town of Boston for a cook who could not only open cans but also make fudge. He said I'd have more important things to do. I must have registered some shock at that statement, but he was quick to reassure me. Said I'd be helping him with ship's accounts and navigation. It was a relief to know that he didn't plan to keep me confined to the bed! Still I wonder. These downeast skippers!

When we arrived from Boston at Aguirre for molasses after a record passage (imagine what the *Boston Herald* will write about Fred making the shortest passage ever on his honeymoon, a trip that might have been purposely prolonged), that nice Mr. McDonald presented me with this notebook for resuming my diary. It seems that I once showed him a part of my old diary in order to prove some point or other about a previous visit, or was it the sailing date of Betty's and mine when we embarked from Aguirre, me as chaperone? Hah!

Anyway, here we are and here is my diary again for me to use as a relief valve when things go wrong or when something happens that should be recorded for explaining to my children the whims and waywardness of their roving parents.

We've had nothing but rain and more rain here in sunny Puerto Rico. But parties, parties, fiestas and fiestas. Everyone has used our wedding for celebrations. The Ponce bomberos, in their red uniforms, met us as we came into Aguirre with a display of their firehoses, spraying streams of water all over Fred's fresh white paint. Scores of acquaintances roasted scores of piglets for the cookouts. I now speak with "oinks" and am so stuffed that friends think I'm pregnant already and, maybe, "had" to get married.

The big bark *Onaway* is anchored astern of us to load after we do, and the crew has been drunk all week on the free rum they swiped at the parties given for Fred and me. They think I'm wonderful. I am, however, no longer a passenger and honored guest. Now I feel like a member of the crew. Washing, cleaning, sewing. What in hell do we have a steward for? What happens if I mutiny?

Wednesday, MAY 17, 1911

Rain! Went to Dona Linda's to get my blue skirt made. Such mud, oh such mud! States mail came on SS *Carolina*, reminding that I once had a ticket to go north on her. Should I have? Heavenly dinner at the Chisholms'. She's no longer trying to pry because she's got a *fait accompli* to think about. One plus, at least.

Thursday, MAY 18, 1911

Never try to predict what a man will do. Today Fred helped me with the washing. Then we took a sailor's holiday by sailing for several hours among the islands and over toward the booming breakers of snowy surf. How Fred loves to sail and so do I. Wouldn't it be perfect if he liked opera, too?

Tuesday, MAY 23, 1911

Went in our launch twenty-nine miles to Ponce as guests of the Kents on board the *Governor Powers*. We're to stay a few days with those lovely people. Fresh milk, so good for my hoped-for little baby.

Wednesday, MAY 24, 1911

Lovely shopping spree in Ponce. New shirts for Fred and lace for me. Went bathing on the *playa* in the afternoon. Wanted to return to the shops for a baby's trousseau, but Fred said it could wait. Please God, all will go well. I do wish Fred wanted a dear little baby as much as I do.

Thursday, MAY 25, 1911

Heavenly dinner of *lechon asado* with all the fixin's at the Melia and later tea at Miss Cudahy's, where I saw all my old friends. Mrs. Groves and Miss Rideout from Boston are dears, and baby Groves is a perfect darling, although Fred seemed afraid of him.

Sewed some of the beautiful Ponce lace on my chemise and then rode to the hills for the evening freshness with Miss Cudahy, who may sail north on the *Powers*. With Captain and Mrs. Kent she should have quite a peaceful trip compared to my chaperonage of Betty and Fred. Jiminy, what a chaperone did yours truly turn out to be! Selah.

Sunday, MAY 28, 1911

Picnic at Caja de Muertos and 18 miles back in the launch. Saw the
Kents and other old friends. Took Miss Cudahy and Miss Ryan along
with two of the young villains from the Central.

   The above entry should have been made for Sunday a week ago.
An indication of my losing a sense of time? Or is it the change from
being an honored (?) guest to being a crew member? The Captain
found fault with my cake frosting and the fudge I made, as he does
with everything I do. Why did I marry? Today went to Merhofs' for
lunch with Alice Hatch as our guest. Later we all went bathing. It
was good to be able to talk with Alice. She was so nice to me in
Boston, showing me around. Reviewing our days there together
helped take my mind off Fred and the frosting and fudge. We talked
of how we took the electric car from Boston to Concord. There is a
powderhouse we saw on the way, at Somerville I believe, containing
cannons used in the Revolutionary and Civil Wars. Its tower flew
the first American flag. We recalled the green at Lexington and
Monroe Tavern, where stands the stone Minuteman commemorating
the first shot heard 'round the world. Then we dined at the Wright
Tavern. My beautiful Concord, so peacefully green, such calmly
dignified trees, oaks and evergreens, and such an air of leisurely
gentleness. And best of all, the Minuteman done by French. He is
leaving the plow and taking up his gun. 'Tis a long retreat they had,
from Lexington to Concord, and so heroic. But what did that
scoundrel of a husband say when he overheard Alice and I
reminiscing? "Good they left Lexington before it was conquered." A
typical fifth-grade, smart-aleck joke. He takes nothing seriously but
ships and food.

   And the Old Manse. Sacred to Hawthorne and Emerson. It is
now in the former's family, and the public are not admitted. Nor did
it seem less human to see a perfectly modern baby carriage on the
lawn in front. Emerson's white, green-shuttered home is also still in
the family. His study is preserved. Further on is the Alcott house

and the Ellentree, now neglected and falling to ruin. God bless the author of *Little Women*! Fred probably thinks they were a group of Panamanian pygmies, like the short San Blas Indians he ships as crew. I wonder if I can ever get him to read some other book than Bowditch, the tide tables, and the ship's log.

Monday, MAY 26, 1911

A perfectly fiendish day! Awful; worked myself to death on not only my wash but also Fred's and half of the steward's tablecloths. Taking medicine and suffering. Ought I to have married?

My new dress is done and is quite suitable. Blue linen. Fred said it made me look good. That's a rare compliment. Downeasters are parted less readily from their compliments than from their money, so I took it that way. I do love my boy, but how cross I get with him at times. Perhaps he needs someone like me who shows a bit of spirit once in awhile. But I do wish the Good Lord would make me a better girl. We have so much.

Wednesday, MAY 31, 1911

Took the track motor to Ponce. Kents gave a party for Miss Cudahy, who definitely sails north with them in the *Governor Powers*. Dinner at the Melia. A heavenly time.

Thursday, JUNE 1, 1911

Back on board the *Hopkins* and slept nearly all day.

Friday, JUNE 2, 1911

Began to load cargo of molasses for Baltimore. Embroidered, read *The Octopus*.

Saturday, JUNE 3, 1911

Bark *Onaway* sailed this morning. Feel like hell with everyone going but us. News came this morning that we're chartered to Rio de Janeiro in September, the usual Christmas cargo Fred and his father seem to have a monopoly on each year. Ice packed in sawdust with barrels of apples on top. Sounds delightful. Will I go, I wonder? Ever since I can remember I've wanted to travel. The years on the farm made it all the more important that I see the big world. Now I have the chance and find myself hesitating just because my big, handsome husband likes his fudge a certain way. Isn't that narrow of me? What's a little longer boiling time for a batch of fudge in comparison with a temper that must be made to boil a bit slower. Why can't I be more like my ancestor, Sir Thomas Moulton, who was written up by Walter Scott in the *Talisman* as being the only one Richard the Lion Hearted could get along with, because Thomas countenanced Richard's high spirits with an even temper? I'll try but it won't be easy, not on your tintype.

Sunday, JUNE 18, 1911

Haven't written in here for two solid weeks. Have been concentrating on Fred, his fudge, and his fusses.

We cleared the ship for the voyage yesterday and may sail tomorrow. Fred is on shore settling up the stevedoring and harbor bills as well as the ship chandlers. Two of the Aguirre boys are going north with us. Spent last evening at Merholfs' and saw good old Doctor Ritter before we left Ponce. Felt better in the cool of the evening after a scandalousy hot day. Dona Lola has finished my sewing, and I picked up all my things Fred asked me to send out to have done. Apparently the fudge has improved; apparently the way to Fred's good graces is through his stomach. Read Elbert Hubbard's writing on James J. Hill. He says, "Pericles built a city but Hill built an empire. He has one credential for greatness: he was born in a log cabin." Little do these easterners understand us from the west and midwest. When I told Fred that my grandfather built a log cabin in Minnesota for his first few winters with his wife, Fred said: "What a waste of good lumber." Bah!

Tuesday, JUNE 20, 1911

Washed today just to show Fred that Monday is not sacred as washday. My next project is to have ice cream on Saturday instead of Sunday and baked beans the reverse. Will the ship sink?

Read some of Keats *Hyperion*. Am I losing all my intelligence and ideals in my petty round of detail? I hope not.

Isn't it a treat to have the fresh pineapples and mangoes and papayas? Does Fred think the way to my good graces is through my stomach? That thought sounds strangely familiar. Could it be that we are, after all, somewhat alike?

Read Woods Hutchinson's article in the *Saturday Evening Post* about the present high standard of American mothers. He's a medical doctor and claims that they excel all former mothers in health, appearance, companionship, ability, and in the small number of children. It has some good thoughts, and one of them is that the writer is an optimist. However, I think he might have offered a bit of evidence, here and there. What does he know about other countries? Does he know that in Latin America marriage is the exception rather than the rule in the lower classes? How could my seamstress, Dona Lola, be healthy, lovely, companionable, able, and the mother of a small family when she has been left by her "husband" with ten children to exist on rice cooked in fat under a leaky roof where the one bed is invaded by him whenever he begs or steals enough to buy a bottle of rot-gut rum and breed another baby?

Wednesday, JUNE 21, 1911 (At sea.)

Washed and ironed. Tea in the afternoon on deck. Read Hubbard's *Little Journey* on Aristotle and how human the latter appears to be.

His boyhood and his friendship with Alexander the Great are emphasized, but very little credit is given to his philosophy. Getting back to Aristotle and away from the phobias of Fred refreshed me and I feel more cheerful.

Thursday, JUNE 22, 1911

The *Carolina* passed across our bow and whistled farewell, three blasts. Little wind. Helped Fred paint the after house a beautiful white. Finished some towels I've been edging. I have been morose, wondering as I worked. Would have been better off reading. I wonder if the washing and painting and other work is too much for me. I hope I shall not be sick. I'd love to go to Rio with Fred. I'd hate having to miss it after having heard and read so much about that glorious city, its diamond necklace about Botafogo Bay and its Copacabana. Fred said he and his father were offered many acres of that beach but decided their money would be better invested in Port Clyde real estate. I think that's like refusing to invest in a proven gold mine.

Longest day of the year, not only by the nautical almanac but by my feelings. Only consolation is that it's the shortest night.

Friday, JUNE 23, 1911

Read *Idle Thoughts of An Idle Fellow*. Not particularly fitting for my present activities, but it's nice to know that there is someone enjoying idleness and making good use of it, as I once did.

Saturday, JUNE 24, 1911

Glory be, I'm pregnant! If a sick pregnancy is a safe one, as some say, I should have a marvelously healthy child. Feel like hell warmed over. If Fred ever ceases to love me, I shall die a natural death. Heigh-ho, nothing can last forever.

Hemmed berth curtains, started a linen pillowslip, and made

two scallops. Wind begins after three days of calm, but in June it's rare to get a spanking sou'wester, which is what we need now that the easterly trades have forsaken us.

Between the old steward, who looks like Punch and hails from Bremen, Germany, and the Saba Island mate, Simmons, who is half Spanish and half pirate, I have begun a most interesting but quite amateurish study of the Spanish and German influence on English sea terms. Coming from them, it's probably unreliable but, then again, it may be more authoritative than some of the ivory-towered dictionary explanations. The Spanish words for bow and poop and boom are respectively *proa*, *popa*, and *pluma*. Stern comes from the German as does deck, ship *(schiff)*, and sail *(segel)*. Starboard is from the Norwegian *styrboard* (steerboard) as marlinspike is from *maalspyk*, or so they say. What richness the English language acquired through robbery. And speaking of robbery, Fred tells me that in his grandfather Hupper's time, the Saba Islanders, like the Nevis men, planted false lights to ground out Maine vessels for ransom. I didn't tell him the story about my Plymouth Colony ancestors importing the notorious pirate, Dixie Bull, in 1631 from England, to smuggle fish and furs from the Penobscot through the French lines to our sacrosanct Pilgrims of the *Mayflower* who prayed for the pirate's success. I found that choice morsel on visiting the Massachusetts Historical Society with Alice Hatch. I shall never tell my mother.

Sunday, JUNE 25, 1911

Fred gave me a dose of sulphur and molasses (we've plenty of the latter) to perk me up this morning when I felt so sick. The result? Felt like death and destruction all day. "Death and decay in all about I see."

Our two passenger-boys are enjoying a lazy trip. Says Wagner: "Oh yes, we're working hard today. It keeps us busy chasing the shade around the house." Says Durchett: "We only get ten hours sleep a night." Says Fred: "They're like Paddy's hurricane: up one mast and down the other."

I envy the boys. Fred frets at not putting them to work but claims they'd upset paint pots and cause more work. He uses an old seagoing expression to describe them: "In everybody's mess (meals) and nobody's watch."

Monday, JUNE 26, 1911

With the rising breeze so rose my spirits. Feel better when going places and so told Fred when he asked me about his idea of buying a farm out west. I have had the life of a farm, and I am most willing to leave it to others.

I figured out the sights today and am beginning to understand navigation, celestial, that is. Fred hasn't the remotest idea of the theory behind it all and I do believe that if his tables were lost we'd sail in circles. I studied his Bowditch, which he calls by the delightful old-fashioned word, "epitome," and in it there's a most lucid explanation of the astronomical triangle. Applying my university course in spherical trigonometry makes it all easy and most sensible. I do believe that with a bit more study I might make up our own tables were they lost. Certainly I can now figure the position with the trigonometric formula given in Bowditch, which is black magic to Fred. However, he always gets us where we're bound, I must say. He says he's from the school of "dog-barking navigators," and when he's along the coast can tell where we are by knowing the difference between the baying of Uncle Isaiah's hound from the snippy bark of Mrs. Gardiner's poodle. Of course, I don't believe him but maybe he's somewhat right in adding what he learned from his father, who never completed grammar school, that some of the best navigating is "by guess and by God." They have both been very successful shipmasters, but I side with Nathaniel Bowditch, who sailed his ship through a fog into Salem Harbor after no sights for three days, so sure was he of his earlier celestial navigation. Selah!

I wonder how it feels to be a man and love a woman and have her for "your wife." Of course I shall never know, anymore than

Fred will never know the astronomical triangle, but I shall ask him. He'll probably just grin.

Tuesday, JUNE 27, 1911

Did my housework today and then had a refreshing salt bath in the beautiful copper tub. Found some gray hairs. Made fudge but not enough for Fred and the two boys. Sails shifted as we changed course slightly westward, now that we're north far enough to no longer fear Cape Hatteras and it's treacherous shoals. Mr. Simmons, the mate, differed with Fred about getting too close to Cape Fear. There were tons of looks that passed between the two but only ounces of words. Reminds me of Captain Kent's story about the whaling Starbuck brothers of Nantucket who had been to sea on one voyage for three years and had become thoroughly uncivil to each other. Captain Starbuck, the older brother, one day, after months of not seeing a whale, congratulated Mr. Starbuck (the mate) on his great good fortune at having harpooned and boarded three large whales in one afternoon. "Have a cigar, Mr. Starbuck," said the Captain. "No thankee, Captain Starbuck," said the mate. "I don't want none of yer seegars." The Captain said, "Then have a noggin of fine Barbados rum, Mr. Starbuck." The mate said, "No thankee, Captain Starbuck. I don't want none o' yer long black Havana seegars nor none of your noggins of rum. All I want from ye, Captain Starbuck, is a little ceevility, and God-damned little o' that."

Wednesday, JUNE 28, 1911

"Not with eye-service as men-pleasers but as servants of Jesus Christ, doing the will of God from the heart." In other words, I had a long, hard night and feel like hell and. . . .

Thursday, JUNE 29, 1911

To take my mind off holy matrimony and unholy sea-captains varnished our cabin deck and finished the embroidery.

pregnant!

"The current flows the way the wind blows," says Mr. Simmons. That in answer to my question about the Gulf Stream starting to veer northeast about here, off the Carolinas. Not believing him I went to Bowditch on tides and currents. The equatorial current from Africa does flow with the easterly trades. Then the stream flows north along the American continent with the prevailing southwest winds until the westerlies start pushing it northeast off the Jersey coast and, later, easterly to Iceland and England, even to Norway where it warms the waters and provides the fish with tropical food. He's not far from right, although I doubt whether he reads any more than does my Fred. Speaking of tropical food, we still have some delicious pineapples and mangoes. Yum!

Friday, JUNE 30, 1911

Made chocolate and did it ever taste good. A miserable night with nausea and pains. Washed and varnished the little after galley, entirely, to put the old steward to shame. He's full of German philosophy and can tell you all about how the Kaiser will chase the English from the seas, but he's dirty, sloppy, and lazy. Came to me with tablecloths that were brown, although they had been washed. He said he had to save water so, "Dey vas soaked and vashed and rinsed all in vun vasser."

Read *The Fall Guy* by Brand Whitlock from an old *Post*. Very good yarn.

Had to get my mind above this ship, because Fred had been talking about Mamie MacPhail. She must have been as low, in mind and politeness, as his others; for all the girls for whom he did so much, giving presents, etc., not one gave us a wedding present. Isn't it strange that even Betty did not, either, after all Fred has done for her. Of course I am selfish even to think of this.

Sunday, JULY 2, 1911

Fred heaved his old shoes overboard to bring wind. A sacrifice to Neptune? It's a tradition going back, I know, and I must spend some

time in re-studying ancient history to see what I can find about
Greek and Roman seamen making their sacrifices to get a fair wind.
Isn't it enchanting?

Calm, calmer, calmest. Shall we ever arrive off the Chesapeake
for Baltimore? I doubt it. Patience, my girl.

Monday, JULY 3, 1911

A little wind. Thanks to the shoes? We are slowly approaching Cape
Henry. Apropos of my being a crew member, the joke Fred likes best
is the one about the colored gentleman before the judge who asked,
"Have you any occupation?"

"Yassuh."

"What is it?"

"I'se the proprietor of a laundry."

"You are? What's its name?"

"Eliza Ann."

I wonder if Eliza Ann received any wages; I don't. But now my
dear, sweet handsome husband with the most beautiful nose says
I'm to be part owner of the *Hopkins*. He's getting me a few sixty-
fourths when we arrive. I'll have the dividends for pin money, he
says. Pin money, be damned! I'll see an opera or two, or should I say
hear an opera?

Tuesday, JULY 4, 1911

Towed up the bay with the *Governor Powers* alongside. Riverview
Park in the afternoon. Iced drinks for a change. Succulent seafood
and a small *despedida* party to the young men from Aguirre.

Wednesday, JULY 5, 1911

Letters. Poor dear sister Nettie, her engagement broken and she is
very tired and sad at home with Mama for a while. A good letter from

Betty. Guess her heart is not broken after all. Saw Captain Kent at agent's office.

Thursday, JULY 6, 1911

Shopped with Fred. Got an icebox for the vessel. Selected a hat and the darlingest pair of blue slippers you ever saw. Fred brought me the daintiest sweet peas and a bunch of yellow coreopsis and some pretty red and white sweet williams. Mrs. Kent came on board in the afternoon and we visited. She is a veteran at sea and sea captains. She said to stand firm and I'd be surprised how they give in.

Fred is sick and we had to cancel our dinner on board the *Governor Powers*. I fed Fred ice cream and cold milk, but Captain Kent said he would call a doctor. There came a Doctor Fiske who did what all doctors do: prescribed rest and a light diet. To bed went Fred with demands for food every hour. No light diet for him!

Monday, JULY 10, 1911

Fred finally better after a long recuperation. Came old friend Linda Deaton, she of Utuado seventh grade fame who passed on to me in the eighth grade those, only those, who could take it. We spent the night on board and she so loved our cabin that she is having her parents fix up a room like our cabin, full of rest and sleep, she says.

Wednesday, JULY 12, 1911

I complain about feeling ill but when Fred gets really sick he says nothing. Wasn't Captain Kent a Godsend. He told me Fred must be watched for his stinginess. Imagine a downeaster saying that! But then it takes one to know one. He sailed as mate with Fred's father, Captain J.W. of the *Mabel Jordan* and now the *Margaret Thomas*, and he tells about Fred as a boy on board. He had a little red tricycle which his father let him ride even in rough weather along the deck.

Fred's mother sailed with her husband for over ten years and then said: "I've served my time and I'm going down home because my home suits me fine." The next trip she wrote her husband that he must have planned the plumbing in their new big house when he was in Rio de Janeiro because the water pipes froze by early December. Captain Kent said she was in Maine even when she was in Rio, refusing strawberries in December because they were out of season. Once, when her husband was too sick to handle the ship and the mate couldn't navigate, she brought the *Mabel Jordan* home to Thomaston from Martinique all by herself. She surely did "serve her time."

Linda and I to Monument Square, and I fairly worshipped the serene grace of the fountains and terraces before partaking of a delicious ice cream soda and buying a melon to take home to Fred. We hope to have Fred's cousin, Roscoe Hupper, Bowdoin and aide to Senator Hale and now studying law in Washington, over for Sunday dinner.

Thursday, JULY 13, 1911 (Washington and Mount Vernon)

Say nothing of the former to me, too much like Minnesota, but of the latter sing me a canto. The pleasant boat ride down the Potomac is a good beginning. You land and climb to meet the Tomb, peaceful and ivy-grown, then the barn of 1733 and the old unpainted family coach. The old kitchen, full of pewter and plate, the fireplace and the eighteen rooms, the exquisite parlor and tasteful bedrooms and small outbuildings nearby for washing, smoking hams, black-smithing, etc. A most pleasing preservation of the old plantation days. In the west we admire Jefferson because he expanded our country so greatly but the downeasters still blame him for ruining their shipping commerce with "Jefferson's War."

Friday, JULY 14, 1911

Tired and feverish after a late arrival home on board last night. Fred never took any medicine the entire time I was away. He believes only in salts, castor oil, and sulphur and molasses, and would probably take one of them for a broken leg. He was feeling mean, and with the crew all paid off, I am the only one about for him to spite. I got some small relief from throwing overboard the little glass paperweight I brought him from Mount Vernon. He swore about it, and I never knew a paperweight could justify so many reasons for nonexistence: it would slide at sea, it was useless, it was a waste of money, it commemorated the "bastard" who caused his greatgrandfather's ships to rot. Maybe he had been drinking. Although I've never see him touch anything but wine, he believes in rum, as do most seamen, as a medicine. Then I discovered that he was thinking me selfish for leaving him alone, which just about broke my heart. Was I? Hope I'll feel better later on. But what a way to show his love, deprecating the poor little paperweight, instead of saying simply that he missed me. However, I now recollect that his highest compliment, like other downeast captains I've met, when thrilled with a choice course at the table, was merely to say to the steward, "It ain't bad." They're afraid a compliment may generate familiarity or laxity or a demand for more pay. Is that a way to treat a wife, even though she's a member of the crew? I shall have to remember the psychology of that for the day when I have to command the ship myself, like Mother B. did.

Saturday, JULY 15, 1911

On board all day, and we finished discharging cargo. Cousin Roscoe writes that he has enough work for ten men to do and cannot come over to visit. Too bad because he and I are the only college graduates in the town of Saint George [Maine]. Fred says Roscoe went to college because he could never learn to sail a ship. I don't believe that. Fred says there's no reason for Saint George boys to go to college unless they want to be preachers, lawyers, or doctors. He says every boy can make a better living going to sea and that college would spoil good seamen, making nothing but a bunch of sea-lawyers, nautical for trouble-makers. Is that thinking akin to the Puerto Rican philosophy of keeping the women barefoot and pregnant?

I did want to go to church tomorrow for the music and the sermon's uplift and to see people, but my boy is so tired and busy I guess I'd better not try it. Also, we may sail this evening and in this heat I'm more comfortable on board.

Sunday, JULY 16, 1911

Did not sail because there is doubt about whether we are chartered to go to Jacksonville. Ice cream made by yours truly in the evening as a special treat for Fred after a bad day working on his pump. Read a good story in the *Post* by a new writer, Melville Davison Post. Purchased *The Inner Shrine*, highly recommended. I hope it is good reading. I need such if we're bound in this heat for torrid Jacksonville.

Monday, JULY 17, 1911

Towed down to Canton Hollow to load gravel ballast. Holds are in a mess and engine needs repairs for pumping and, later, hoisting sails. Fred on shore all morning. Our new engineer, the third in less than two weeks, thinks he owns more of this ship than does Fred. I hope he won't be too bossy when Fred returns, because Fred will throw him ashore in no time. The way the engineer tries to boss the mate around is a caution. He will learn. Oh, he will learn when Fred gets back. Fred remembers his grandfather telling him of the donkeys that were carried on the olden-day ships to run continously around the capstan shaft, below deck. Hence the term "donkey engine" when vessels finally displaced the poor animals, some of which were blinded, with steam. He still calls an engineer "donkeyman" when he wants to put him in his place.

Have been writing letters. And told my mother of the wisdom of sailors, how today there came on board a package of chiclets, chewing gum for me, and the mate put them in the engineroom for repairing leaks in the pump. Oh me, oh my! And Fred says they don't need education!

Tuesday, JULY 18, 1911

Began reading *The Inner Shrine* yesterday. Took a snap of the bay this morning. A card from Linda, thanking us. Must write her.

Thanks be, the pump is finally sucking water and has caught the rising water in the hold at last. But just as it did — oh irony or fate! — the steam pressure from the donkey engine went down. We were flooded until Fred and the engineer got steam up and now we're out of trouble.

The old steward goes on and on about how such wouldn't have happened on Captain J.W.'s *Margaret Thomas*. For him there's no ship like her and no skipper like Captain J.W. He has even been heard by me to say "Dat dom Fred," an allusion to the years Fred served as mate to his father when the old steward would hear their Starbuck-like interchanges. Fred likes to have the old steward with us because he's a wonderful cook and says he'll be alright when we get to sea and away from the Pabst beer which must be loaded with Dutch courage.

The steward is an old devil, but looks like Puck with his beery smile covering that cherubic face under the tipsy derby, and he loves to sweetly belittle Fred by reminding him in front of me how little Fred used to ride his red tricycle about the decks of the *Margaret Thomas*. He fairly swooned with pleasure yesterday when I told Fred, who was bothering me, to go ride his tricycle. Fred could not utter a word in reply, and I thought he was shocked, surprised,

chagrined, and grieved but finally out came that slow, lovely smile
for which I married him as well, of course, as for his nose and a
chance to roam the world. J.P. Morgan's yacht, the *Corsair*, passed
down the bay yesterday and me thinks he has nothing on little me. I
can live like a millionaire, on this beautiful four-masted yacht of
mine, without being one. I cannot understand why Mother B. says
she's served her time at sea and goes no more with Captain J.W. But
then, anyone who refuses to eat those luscious strawberries in Rio
de Janeiro because they're out of season back home in Maine doesn't
have a chance to enjoy the big world.

Wednesday, JULY 19, 1911

Still lying at anchor, and I am full of ennui. We've pumped the
whole of Chesapeake Bay through this ship. But I always feel blue on
the dark of the moon. Went ashore yesterday with a feeling of "oh
boy, oh joy" but almost fainted when the physician said I was not
pregnant but had eaten too many soft-shelled crabs. Bought a black
leather handbag to console me, and how I do enjoy swinging it like
any sailor's dolly.

Was to meet Fred at the Crown for lunch, but the handbag
delayed me and I was late. He worried a heap, bless him. Hired a
launch and went aboard just as he was arriving. Had words with him
and now I dread the Jacksonville trip as well as the terrible heat
down there. Wish we could get to the other side of the Gulf Stream,
such as Europe where our American stream moderates the
European climate. On this side of the stream it's either too hot or
too cold. Fair France does not go to such extremes.

Spent the afternoon adding to my compilation of sea-going
lingo; a holiday is a spot left unpainted; sou'westers, the heavy
weather hats, get the name from England where dirty weather comes
from the southwest, from the Gulf Stream; channel fever comes
from England, too, where all hands changed their outlook when
coming home and approaching the English channel; skoweigan, the
name for a Scandinavian, is a comical mixture of skow with
Norweigan; schooner-rigged means a sparcity of belongings and

derives from the full-rigged sailors' disdain for the lightness of the number of sails on a schooner; Uncle Sam's crow is the United States eagle on the stamp of custom's documents; Ali Baba and the Forty Thieves are the custom's officials who have been known to confiscate precious but hidden bottles. It's a language unto itself. The animal kingdom enters strongly into the speech of men who seldom see animals. A heaving line is thrown with a monkey's fist; a decorated knot is a catspaw; a back splice is, heavens be, a dog's cock; a knot to hold a line on a gangway is a Turk's head; ratlines are part of the standing rigging; holding the anchor from paying out is a claw. An incompetent seaman "ain't worth a fart in a gale of wind"; a deaf one "can't hear himself fart." Poor, dear Mama, pray for your wayward daughter! To heave a line in just a bit is "a cunt's hair." What good books have you read lately, Dorothea?

Thursday, JULY 20, 1911

On shore today where we lunched with Captain Smith of Bath on, of all things, soft-shelled crab. Heard several captains say how able and "smart" (meaning competent) was my boy who looked "some old elegant" (downeast for good) in his new blue suit. I had made him get it. He cares nothing for dress. The old steward often tells and tells again how disgusted Captain J.W. used to be with Fred who would, when forced to put on a necktie, adorn his neck with a ropeyarn. But oh he's a darling boy. He had the ship chandler throw into the stores for the trip some grape juice and some malted milk for me so I could stand the Florida heat. Won't it taste good at sea! Won't it just! Must write brother Roy out in dismal Minnesota and poor Betty Holbrook before we sail. Must be careful to use their English instead of my sea-going lingo. Altogether incomprehensible to them, and overly graphic.

Friday, JULY 21, 1911

I have sea fever, want to get sailing and use my newly acquired ability, on paper at least, to take longitude sights. But on shore we did go again early in the morning and over to Druid Hill Park, where the thick grass felt good under my bare feet. Lunched at the Crown with Mr. Washburn of Thomaston, part owner of the *Hopkins*, the *Fred B. Balano* (three-master), the *Carrie T. Balano*, the *John Balano*, and the *J.W. Balano*, all valuable vessels that do well for him and our family. Fred could stay ashore and help run the fleet, but he'd rather go to sea and so would I. It's better than living back in Squeedunk.

Saw the big collier *Neptune* go down the Bay this morning. Carries 13,000 tons of coal. I suppose we'll have to get into steamships, but both of us dread it. Such smoke and living high above the water instead of down below in our cozy cabin. We both detest rust buckets, but apparently they're here to stay, damn them. Our comfy cabin is cool and one hears the sea go by.

Saturday, JULY 22, 1911

L'envoi, happy days, towing down the Bay with a Curtis Bay tug groaning ahead of us. Letter from Mama telling me she worries and hoping I can visit her during Chautauqua season when "many wonderful preachers will come from as far away as Boston." Thanks, Mama, but I think I'll just sail.

Beautiful nor'west wind. Wish we were clear of the Capes and bowling along at sea. Chautauqua! Bah!

Sunday, JULY 23, 1911

No wind and anchored all morning off Cape Henry. I asked Fred if he didn't have another pair of old shoes for throwing overboard to make a sacrifice for wind to the Gods. Says Fred: "I don't know nawthin' about sacrifices to the Gods. I threw them shoes overboard because I've seen the oldtimers do it. Besides, they said not to do it too often or it wouldn't work. I'll save my old clothes for when we really need a breeze." And sure enough, about noon a fair wind sprang up, and we sailed merrily out to sea steering "by the wind," that is, with the wind just aft of the beam.

Read *The Brass Bowl*, a right interesting burglar yarn by Louis Vance who knows just what I want in a sensational story.

Made Currituck Light by dark and passed Bodie Island in the night. I took four-point bearings and plotted our distance off in order to get a good departure for my morning longitude sights. I'll try to cross the pole star for latitude with Arcturus and Capella for longitude, and that should give a good fix. The stars are hardly visible by naked eye just before sunrise, but they're here for anyone to see who has the good fortune to see bits of the universe through a sextant.

The old steward made delicious doughnuts and I sewed. I want a sewing machine and will see to it that I get one.

Tuesday, JULY 25, 1911

Wind died yesterday and we were still on soundings so we anchored at four P.M. Saw Cape Hatteras at dark. At anchor all night and how this ship did roll in the seaway. I ought to write some letters, but it's more fun fishing as we did last night with lights over the stern to attract the schools of mackerel.

Hoisted sails at six A.M. and are headed south with just enough breeze to give us steerageway. At nine we sighted Hatteras Lightship and steered close by, within a heaving-line's distance, so as to ask them to report us as they have wireless. Fred told about the neophyte captain of a tugboat who had come down to saltwater from the Great Lakes and was on his first trip out of Boston to solicit tows of sailing ships up into the harbor. Never having seen a lightship, he went alongside of the Boston Lightship and sang out, "You want a tow? Only fifty dollars." The lightship skipper yelled, "You damn fool, this is a lightship." Said the innocent: "Don't make no difference, light or loaded, it's fifty dollars." Of course, I don't believe that for one instant. It's just saltwater disdain for freshwater men. It's like Fred saying there are two kinds of Maine people; the coastal ones are called sea maniacs, he says, and the interior tribe are swamp maniacs.

Thursday, JULY 27, 1911

Washed today, damn it. Used the little ship's boiler for the first time. Of washing, Fred said his mother used to berate the old steward who would proudly come aft with Fred's clean diapers and, proud at saving water on a long trip, boast that the intimate baby garments had been "vashed and rinzzed und den boiled all in vun vassser." *La plus ca change!*

Passed Cape Lookout Lightship at noon today. Twelve schooners in company with us, all bound south and, I dare say, all praying after their own fashion for a good wind to get around Frying Pan Shoals. Fred says the bottom hereabouts is so thick with hurricane-murdered ships that one could walk underwater on them without touching bottom.

My clothes look lovely, and as they hang on the line over the cabin in the sun to dry seem to attract more attention from the crew than they might receive from landsmen, who see such things more frequently than seamen. To the crew they have all the oddness of a zoo.

Finished all the sewing on my linen corset cover and shall proudly change the M on it for a fancy embroidered B. Selah.

Heard a new one today. The second mate disputed with Fred about the course laid out for clearing Frying Pan Shoals. Seems Fred had given the mate one course and he gave another to the man at the wheel. Fred took the mate into the chartroom to prove his point, gently and without the usual brawling. That was too much for the second mate, who is not accustomed to kind words. The worthy then said, "Either course will get us there." Fred had exhausted his rare attempt to persuade instead of order. "Don't give me none of your God-damned back-slack," I heard him say as they emerged. After a bit of thought, I figured it out. When heaving or pulling on a rope with a winch or capstan, the slack must be taken up or there will be rope under foot, snarls and dangerous backlash, possibly. So, to a sailor, an uncalled-for reply is backslack. I asked Fred to substantiate my theory, and he just looked at me. "Why do you bother your pretty head with that stuff," he said. "I dunno where it come from. All I know is backslack's no good." My intellectual lover-boy!

Friday, JULY 28, 1911

Two hundred and seven miles to Jacksonville according to my sights at dawn. Two hundred according to Fred's. Finished ironing after breakfast and my back is broken. Eleven other schooners in sight. Wonder what happened to the twelfth. When I took my sights, I proudly told Fred I had shot Capella, using his sea-going expression. "Poor bastard, Capella," said Fred, "I hope you just wounded him." Mercy, what a childish sense of humor.

Saturday, JULY 29, 1911

I knew from the remark about Capella that foul weather was brewing in the head of my sometimes ugly love. Sure enough today he started talking about Betty again. Have I displeased him? I do wish he would stop it, even though he may just be letting off steam at being bound to just one woman after his career of the forty-one plus. I hope that notorious skirt-chaser, Captain Kent, has not influenced my boy toward going to other women. Then, I suppose he wouldn't be a good sailor if he didn't. Do I pray or swear? Swearing will be more effective with him. I'll swear. At least I no longer will have to search for the proper profanity to use. I've memorized it all, with right emphasis.

Did Fred's ties and made some fudge. Wrote friends in Ponce. Caught a lovely mackerel so enormous Fred had to help me land it over the rail. Fresh fish for supper and wouldn't you know it! The steward made dumplings to go with the fish, *knodel*. I'm slowly picking up some German for when we sail to Europe, God willing.

Sunday, JULY 30, 1911

Fred says he'll take me to Bremen, Maine, where German is still spoken by the German settlers sent over by the Hanoverian kings. He says around Waldoboro, the Genthners, Branns, Simmons and Manns have kept up some German, among the old folk. I told him how nice that was, but I was thinking more of Bremen, Germany. He told me to speak to Mr. Thurlow and Mr. Washburn, the managers of the charters. Believe you me I shall do just that.

Another mackerel caught last night and wasn't it some delicious for breakfast this morning. I said that the steward had told me it was a Spanish mackerel. Fred said he didn't hear the mackerel talk. For that I should have slapped the mackerel in his face, the dear darling strong sea-captain with the humor of a sixth-grader.

Read the August *Cosmopolitan* today and certainly enjoyed the yarn by C.N. Buck about the playwright — the Queen Bee — Dimity and Butler.

After a calm morning, there is a good breeze this evening, thanks be. Only about 180 miles to go. Roast chicken for dinner and how good it does taste at sea. Our coop still contains four chanticleers, which try their best to wake me before dawn for star sights, bless them. Fred says he and I will get all the eggs those roosters lay this trip; none for the crew. My boy, my boy!

Monday, JULY 31, 1911

Washed clothes again, again, and again, and all through by 10:30. Used carbon paper to help embroider my corset cover. Linen all made up, praise the Lord. Consumed an entire bottle of grape juice in the heat. It'll be much hotter on land. How I dread the land when it's unpleasant. No channel fever for me this trip, so long as the grape juice lasts.

Wednesday, AUGUST 2, 1911

Just love the way Fred wakes me up in the morning. "Dode, little Dode, wake up." And then a kiss. "Dode, it's time for you to take the sights and tell me where we are." More loving. Then the stars, the figuring, the comparison of his sights with mine, compromises on just exactly where we are. Then a tale, the latest about how when Fred was second mate he'd use the point of a pencil to show his father precisely, within a heaving-line's distance, of their position. When he was mate he matured a bit and wasn't quite so sure of the pencil-point position, so he'd put his thumb on the chart and say they were about there, within a twenty-mile radius. "When I got my own ship I used the palm of my hand, covering fifty miles and I'd say that's where we are."

Heigh-ho, why can't I have breakfast after sights instead of waiting until seven o'clock? Why am I always hungry at sea?

Only eighty miles to go, and that's not bad what with all the headwinds we had.

Thursday, AUGUST 3, 1911

Passed two lights last night, Brunswick, Georgia and Ferdnandina, Florida. Only about fifteen miles to go, but the wind was contrary during the night and we had to run out to the east. A towboat is in sight, probably out from Ferdnandina, and she may be here to pick up the *Bertram*, Captain Pinkham, sailing astern of us and bound for Ferdnandina for railroad ties.

My new linen drawers are turning out beautifully now, all stitched by hand, damn it. They're saucy. Wonder how soon we shall arrive off Jacksonville. Despite the damnable heat of the Godforsaken place, I hope it will be soon so I can get it over with the quicker.

Pilot at ten minutes after midnight and the tugboat *Three Friends*. Fred said he didn't need her yet, not at fifty dollars, but to come back when we got farther in and we'd pay thirty. They settled at forty dollars. Downeast trickery! We towed up the Saint John's river and went ashore. Jacksonville is a new, quite modern city with wide streets, a white marble post office, and quite different from the other southern towns, which are older and show it. 'Tis said of some of these southerners that they do not know the Civil War has ended. This city does. It owes its growth and prosperity to Yankee markets and ingenuity. All of the 75,000 inhabitants seem to have more "git up and git" than most southerners. But it's still hellishly hot.

Had supper on shore at the Metropolitan, fried young chicken and cantaloupe. Umm, were they good! Am beginning to think more highly of Jacksonville.

Friday, AUGUST 4, 1911

Went from the anchorage to the dock this morning, but it did take forever and we couldn't discharge ballast because it rained and poured so hard that no stevedores would work. Received a $25 dividend from Boston for my share in the vessel's recent profits. Isn't Fred too dear for words. I suppose so, but let me choose the words.

One of our colored crew members got quite mouthy, and I see trouble on the horizon. All he needs is half a chance and perhaps a trip ashore to a rum shop. Cleaned the lamp chimneys, finished embroidering a pair of lovely panties and wrote two letters. Feel enormously valiant and self-satisfied as I hate those kinds of work.

Sunday, AUGUST 6, 1911

Church this morning but only the songs were familiar, not the minister or the people, and it seems strange to go to a church where you don't see familiar faces; but that's a small price to pay for travel. I don't suppose I shall see many familiar faces at Saint Peter's when we do get to Rome, and we shall, by golly. Am I tiring of roaming so soon? Do I want to settle down and gather moss and a few friends *tambien* (Editor's note: tambien is Spanish for "as well").

The Erbs called and stayed on board for supper. They have a darling little girl baby, who set me thinking. Cantaloupe for breakfast and, Jimminy, wasn't it good.

Monday, AUGUST 7, 1911

My housework done by 8 A.M. Hot today. Fred has gone over town.

Later — Had the best day. Went on board the SS *Algonquin* of the Clyde Line, Captain Charles Devereux of Castine. The gruff but gracious Captain Charles showed us all about his passenger steamship and I weakened just a bit in my determination to have Fred always stay in sail. Such lovely accommodations. Met two charming southern belles, friends of the Captain, and had the most delicious lunch with ice cream and lemonade. Met several Maine skippers and some of their wives at the Metropolitan. Of the seven vessels loading in the port, five are Maine schooners. The men talked of ships and shoes and the women of sealing wax, while I sat by, making mental notes but wishing Jacksonville had a light opera or opera theater. Do I inherit the contrary streak that sent my ancestors continually away from civilization, always westward from Plymouth Colony, first to Vermont, then upstate New York, and then to Minnesota?

Tuesday, AUGUST 8, 1911

Housework, sewing, pressed Fred's clothes, made fudge.

Letter from Betty Holbrook. She's still at home in Montana and not feeling well. Wish she had sense enough to buck up and be beautiful again.

1 P.M. Captain Darrah of Maine for dinner and supper. We took him for a launch ride along the river in the evening. Stopped at the

landing of the Erb farm and saw their ostriches. Ugly birds and make such queer noises; the Australians can have them.

Wednesday, AUGUST 9, 1911

I'd stay in Jacksonville so long as the delicious cantaloupes hold out, no longer. Shall I go to town or sew? Really it's too hot to move. Went over town because tomorrow we shift to the loading dock, and that will give me a chance to iron and wash, because it's too far from the center of town and I would have to walk too far to the streetcar to get to town. Isn't that lovely thinking for getting out of work?

Mrs. Erb called, without her ostriches. Her baby is a dear. Miss Foote came on board for tea and spent the evening under a magnificent moon. Aren't Florida watermelons good!

Friday, AUGUST 11, 1911

Towed downriver to the lumber dock this morning. Towboat came at 5:30 A.M. We're loading for Beverly, Massachusetts, with a few thousand feet for Boston. The Beverly cargo is for building a wharf there. Letters galore! Linda Deaton sent the photos of Washington and Mount Vernon. Those of the bark *Onaway* and the Kents' party in Ponce came out foggy. Sister Nettie wrote from Minneapolis where she teaches, *tambien*. She's a natural spinster, shooing away the men by lecturing to them. Two broken engagements already. When will she learn to stop *metiendo la pata* (Editor's note: Spanish for putting one's foot in one's mouth).

Had a lovely, unexpected little drive with my Freddie boy this morning out of Jacksonville to the upper country where the alligators thrive and the palms are thicker than four in a bed. How I enjoyed it! Home on board to sew on my nightie, the new lace, and isn't it lovely.

On board the sistership to this one in the evening. Wonderful moon during the launch ride. Captain Hooper is very kindly. He used to take Fred on board as a boy. The old skipper has the square, strong hands of a sailor and the smilingest blue eyes one ever discovered behind tanned and crows-footed eyelids.

Saturday, AUGUST 12, 1911

Uptown this morning and at home all P.M. Dreadfully hot. Fred says I complain of the heat only when there's no place to go. Read *The Common Law* and sewed on another new corset cover. All finished but the embroidery, which I started. Walked over to the Grand in the cool of the evening and took in some good moving pictures. Had ice cream afterwards and walked back aboard. My darling boy was a bit under the weather but is getting better. Made fudge for him to gobble. He eats it with both hands.

Sunday, AUGUST 13, 1911

Thought I'd give the Presbyterians a look-over this morning. Young minister, old songs. Home to read *Ethan Frome* by Mrs. Wharton in *Scribners*. Do wish I could get all of the coming numbers and read the entire novel. Does bid to be good. New England supplies the local color and, God knows, "we Yankees" have plenty of that. How's that for a transplanted farmer girl who has spent all of a week in Maine? But then, this ship is but an extension of Herring Gut (Editor's note: until the late 1800s, Port Clyde was known as South Saint George and the village at the tip of the peninsula was on Herring Gut harbor).

Monday, AUGUST 14, 1911

Washed clothes till hell won't have it. Raineth it always in Jacksonville? Oh Lordy, how my back does ache. P.M. Fred uptown. I hate to think of the gossip relayed to us by some about a certain Captain's wife. It makes a bad taste in my mouth, which even the cantaloupes and watermelons can't cancel. Hope it is not true. Our launch being repaired and hope it's soon ready for evening cruises along the river. Thus we seafarers take our holidays.

Tuesday, AUGUST 15, 1911

More gossip. How could she possibly give herself to the mate? Is her husband blind or does he drink? What a shame and what a bad thing for the reputation of the profession, where most of the wives are wonderful.

Washed clothes again today and ironed until it tired me furiously. Then for a launch ride in the evening and took along Captain Farrar. The Pilot Boat stopped us to inspect, but we had the required rules on board the launch. Several launches have been fined.

Wednesday, AUGUST 16, 1911

Sick in bed all morning. Fred called a doctor and, woe is me, they made yours truly get up. No rest for the wicked, pain or no pain. Heighho, the pleasant launch ride in the afternoon was good medicine and better was the long one at eventide down to where the *Hy. J. Smith*, is anchored in the stream below town. The Moores were not on board, so we went on board Captain Darrah's vessel to see his good pictures of ports, ships, and his fine family. Home to lemonade and so to bed.

Friday, AUGUST 18, 1911

Ironed yesterday and sick today, or is it sick of ironing? First real bust-up with Fred, and of today's events, the shouting, the pettiness, the empty anger, which I shall never forget, nothing will be said. But I'll not forget if I live to be a thousand years. Says Fred, among other things, "You're soldiering." That's sea talk for loafing. Says I: "I didn't sign on for being a Chinese laundry."

"Is it the heat that's getting you, Fred darling?" The "darling" with disgust on my gritting teeth, "Or is it drinking?"

"Damn it, you know I don't drink."

"Sipping, then. I smell it".

"You're some old educated smart, ain't you. That's medicine you smell."

"Some call it that," says I.

He was furious and went into the virtues of several Mollies, a Mary, and two or three unknown trollops whose backs are apparently stronger than their minds.

"If all you want is your clothes ironed and your sex appetites satiated, then bring aboard one of your Boston dollies and I'll pack my bag. I'll bet she won't be able to navigate outside of the bunk."

"Saysheate! What in hell is that? Don't go showing off in front of me."

And so on until he said something that made me laugh.

"You couldn't be sick if you tried. You're just lazy as hell when we're in port. That's just fine for a sailor's girl."

Then, of course, I felt worse for having needled him. And when he called the doctor, I broke down at his great love for me.

Monday, AUGUST 21, 1911

If all goes well, I shall sit up *manana*. Am now enjoying the lovely grapes my darling husband brought me. Today came a bundle of Portland papers to read this evening. Kaiser Bill seems bound and determined to force a war by building a stronger navy than the British.

Tuesday, AUGUST 22, 1911

Sat up while Fred made my bed. Aren't clean sheets a luxury. Wrote sister Nettie. Read the best polo match story in the *American* magazine. Wonder if Fred would like it. I'll probably have to read it to him. He doesn't like to read anything but charts.

Wednesday, AUGUST 23, 1911

Up on my feet and now tending Fred's rheumatism, which
sometimes cripples him. Shipchandler left a note to call his office,
44744. I went up the dock and rang up. The operator said, "Foe-foe-
seven-foe-foe, right smart of foes, lawzy mercy honeychile."

The message was that Captain Darrah wanted to visit us, which
he did with some so-called poetry written by two girls he and Mrs.
Darrah took for a trip at sea.

Ask me not in mournful numbers
Of my passage on the sea
Ask me not if I was sea-sick
Such words don't sound good to me.

For that effort I'd give an eighth-grader a flunking mark. Guess
I'll have to stop encouraging such exhibitions, as I may do with
speaking so that the sea-captains know I managed to go beyond
seventh grade. When they discover that I like poetry, they bring me
doggerel.

From the other sea-captains, all suffering from rhuematism,
like Fred, I've run a pseudo-scientific research questioning, and the
results may be that they can no longer justifiably blame it on the
weather. I believe their rheumatism results from their extremely
high salt intake. Seamen eat salt fish, salt pork, corned beef, and
oodles of canned food, which has high sodium content. They breath
salt, bathe in salt, and cover their food with it, even when no salt is
necessary. Shall I write my theory to John Hopkins? No, better wait
until I determine how Fred does after I've hidden the salt shaker;
had the cook boil the salt out of the fish, pork, and beef, and am
trying to convert him to eating rice. That'll take some doing, my
daughter. He loves salt. Even says that when he retires to that
illusory and damnable farm, he will salt away his earnings, a layer of
one dollar bills, a layer of salt, and so on until the barrel's full and
topped with salt.

My pseudo-scientific endeavors have been otherwise diverse during this stay in Jacksonville, stimulated by finding out that the Captain I've been calling Darrow spells his name Darrah. Then we met a Mr. Tolliver whose name is spelled, lo and behold, Taliaferro. The downeast Delanos are called Dilno. The Balanos name is pronounced Blaino. Why can't these easterners forget their English heritage with its notorious disdain for spelling? Imagine getting Chumley out of Chomondeley! It's as bad as Wooster from Worcester and Gloster from Gloucester. All this by way of having heard that Captain Darrah's rheumatism (salt intake) has finally caught up with him, and he's to be shipped home while a new skipper is being sent down from Maine to sail the *Lewiston* home.

Sunday, SEPTEMBER 3, 1911

To sea at last. Praise the Lord. Am I ever fed up with the picayune peccadillos of the stay in this gunkhole. Won't the sea breezes refreshingly blow away the cobwebs! Oh, a few retrieving episodes did happen to take the curse away. Fred's Uncle Sid Hupper of Herring Gut and skipper of a big schooner came on board with a large bundle of *Rockland Couriers*, got myself the new *Scribners* and *Outlook*, wore my pongee dress to church, where the young minister read my thoughts by quoting, "The mills of the Gods grind slowly, but they grind exceedingly small, tho with patience stands he waiting, with exactness grinds he all." Had egg and wine one lunchtime. My precious darling husband got more and more affectionate, which mood usually precedes a fight. Many women wonder why that happens, but I can be true to my diary and tell exactly why. It's simply that the husbands are leading up to copulating and with that they'd like a bit of fellatio, lacking which they get nasty and start a battle. He even went so far as to tell me I might not make the forthcoming trip to Rio de Janeiro. Come hell and high water I'll be in Rio for Christmas! And he can battle all the way. I shall not be a fellatrix, Captain, oh my Captain, and if that be mutiny, make the most of it.

Ate beautiful oysters, large and pink and white, while towing down the river. And the farewell gift of potted hydrangeas is lovely enough to dispel my wrath. The lumber people paid Fred for two day's demurrage (Editor's note: demurrage is a delay beyond charter party time stipulations). Please God no hurricane, for this is the season when they blow poor ships astray and sink them. But at least they provide wind and that's what we want, up to a point. And if anyone can take advantage of the wind before the eye of the hurricane makes sailing impossible, it's Freddie boy, the sailor who says an ancestor of his showed Noah how to knot a ropeyarn. Passed the SS *Cretan*, Merchants and Miners, in bay.

Monday, SEPTEMBER 4, 1911

Wind failed last night and had to anchor. Towed down this morning by the tug *Biscayne* as the *Three Friends* was broken down, a bit more than usual.

Washed!

How hungry I get since following Fred's foolish prescription of turpentine and castor oil. Believe you me I shall get a doctor's manual when we reach Boston, right out of the Harvard Medical School, and put a stop to his doctoring with nostrums.

Shall I get a new gown and long coat in Boston or a suit and silk waist? Am I going to be seasick with the confounded turpentine and castor oil? I never have been seasick and that's one reason I'm here, poor Betty. Wonder if I should tell Harvard, if they balk on the manual, that my ancestors, both Moulton and Brewster, helped found the damnedly noble institution.

Wednesday, SEPTEMBER 6, 1911

A beautiful sou'east breeze yesterday. Fred lame but dousing his Florida celery in salt and I embroidering on deck. Cloudy today and just a day for soogying (Editor's note: washing with soap powder) the after cabin, which is what the sailors are doing. I see from the *Saturday Evening Post* that while my back was turned New Mexico became a state. President Taft has vetoed their attempt to provide recall of undesirable officials, says the *Post* in an overly righteous lecture down to the westerners, who it is said are called by easterners "Sons of the braying jackass."

Thursday, SEPTEMBER 7, 1911 (Off Cape Fear)

A squall upset a bucket of green paint atop the house, and that makes Fred happy because the sailors were running out of work.

My blue drawn dress is ready to wear again but shan't put it on until we have passed fearful Cape Hatteras. Fred washed the cabin overhead, groaning all the time with his aches and pains while I lectured him on "soldiering." That's what kept him going with a grin between groans. Ironed and pressed Fred's clothes in the galley, where there's plenty of hot water and finished sewing on little sister Myra's surprise pillow, very pretty. Had a beautiful sunset of opal and pale blue, just a weather-breeder says Fred, while we were strolling fore and aft in the lee of the house as though we were doing the Strand in Londontown.

Saturday, SEPTEMBER 9, 1911

Only light airs for two days and how this ship did roll fiendishly and pitch diabolically so one could hardly sleep. Undoubtedly and with absolute certainty we are near Hatteras. No charts or lights or lightships are necessary to ascertain that fact, just the movement of the ship as the shoal meets the deep; the Gulf Stream protests the long shallows and the trades battle the westerlies into a contrary draw of winds, which are calm one minute and squally the next. Began on a linen pillow for Mother B. Fred finished varnishing the cabin walls and deck. The sea became calm during the evening and threateningly beautiful.

Sunday, SEPTEMBER 10, 1911

Calm, calmer, calmest. We make no money this way but 'twas perfectly heavenly when the slight breeze started about noon, and I am glad to have the rest and do some letters. Began *Saracinerea* by F. Marion Crawford and isn't it splendid. His characters are well drawn, strong, and vital. Fred went to bed early with pain, and I made him take aspirin. I read until the duel took place and went to sleep with nightmares; and Fred, too, of course. Isn't it lovely to have one's own man to hold when the going is not too good! Especially when there are four in the bed: Fred, his pain, my nightmare, and me.

Monday, SEPTEMBER 11, 1911

Very calm until noon, when came a fair wind for Nantucket, which is still over four hundred miles north by east. Grey, chilly northern sky, such as leadened Betty and me just out of sunny Puerto Rico over a year ago. Wonder if the dear child is snapping out of it, writing her Life and, I hope, teaching amongst a flood of eligible beaux. She wouldn't have made it with this one, not tough enough.

Just had some grape juice and egg for breakfast — but are they ever good together!

Fred missed morning sights. Said: "I'll trust you. Let the mate take sights, too. His won't be any good but you can compare them with yours." The mate was all thumbs, handling the delicate sextant as though scared of it. He puts us somewhere up in the Alleghenies. "Hard sailing up there," said Fred when I took him the results, "Reminds me of the drunken fisherman of Metinic who couldn't stand numbers, couldn't count. Came home to the mainland one night to sell his lobsters and thought he'd climb in bed with his wife for a change. Drunk, he pulled up the blanket, no sheets of course, and counted six feet. Thought something was wrong.

Jumped out on the floor and counted only four feet. Hopped back in and said, 'Four feet, that's all there should be.' " Is that another downeast lie?

Tuesday, SEPTEMBER 12, 1911. (Still, yet, and evermore.)

Ironed.
Starched.
Washed companionway.
Damn them all!
Finished that splendid *Saracinerea* by Crawford, who is not a lazy writer, like me. He knows history and is a consummate handler of vital characters. I want to read his next, *Sant Ilario*.

Wednesday, SEPTEMBER 14, 1911

Alas and alack for human hopes. Had a lively sou'west wind last evening, just where it should be, which promised to get us in within a few days, but in the night there blew up a raging nor'easter, chasing the sou'wester back to the Gulf and us off our course, and here we are somewhere between Greenwich and Hawaii, God knows where. Just tacked ship to get back on course for Nantucket but not doing too well close-hauled. Passed two six-masters southbound and a steamer, which shows we are in the right direction for Nantucket Lightship. Fred put his whole palm on the chart and said, "We're near here." Too overcast for sights, so we'll navigate "by guess and by God" until the sun pops out. Fred's hand covers nearly two hundred miles radius.

Thursday, SEPTEMBER 14, 1911

Headwinds out of the northwest all night. Passed several steamers, or they passed us, and now a three-master is following us astern.

Nearly finished a sofa pillow. To have a new hat in Boston or not to
have, that is the question.

Tacked at four bells in the afternoon and got a sounding of 47
fathoms; lard on the lead showed sandy bottom. In closer than we
thought toward land so tacked offshore on a northeast course but
made little seaway in the calm.

Friday, SEPTEMBER 15. (Somewhere north of Nantucket Lightship but south of Cape Cod.)

Had thought of writing Betty a note, but if I did would say that for
her own sake I was thankful she was not here and she might
misinterpret that. Her feelings might be hurt. The best way out is to
write nothing but get done with "soldiering" and wash the overhead
of the messroom, which I prefer to call the dining room.

Said task is only half done and it is evening. Do not feel very
well. The world sometimes goes around before my eyes.

Cape Cod Light is flashing off on the port bow and we have a
good breeze. Shall it be Beverly tomorrow?

Saturday, SEPTEMBER 16, 1911

Heading in the wrong direction, running for Nova Scotia as fast as
this wind will take us. Too cloudy, dark, and foggy to haul up for
tricky Boston Bay. Then, near noon, with the wind decreasing, we
hauled in a bit more westerly, then sou'west and finally heard Cape
Cod's foghorn: a blast lasting eight seconds. Very foggy. The mate
said: "It's clear overhead, Captain." The Captain said, "We ain't
goin' that way, not just yet."

With all the running abouts, handling sails, I marvelled at one
crew member, a little, squat San Blas Indian Fred picked up off
Panama. While the West India blacks and the Matthews County
boys from Virginia would climb up and down the ratlines to shift the
gaskets and lines for the topsails, little Jackson calmly walked from
mast to mast on the stays, ninety feet above the deck, his broad, bare

feet manipulating the narrow stays as though they were padding along a forest trail.

Very calm now and thick of fog. Soundings gave us fifty-five fathoms at one P.M. The bottom is rocky and broken, like me.

Am too discouraged and so permeated with this deadening peasoup fog that I can't do anything; even letters are a bore.

Sunday, SEPTEMBER 17, 1911. (Somewhere off Cape Cod. Somewhere!)

Thirteen days out of Jacksonville today, one of the slowest passages my boy ever made and is he sick about it! Laid-to all last night and rolled, but it was good to have my poor, tired boy get a good night's sleep for a change.

At dawn the fog lifted a bit and showed us Cape Cod Lighthouse on Race Point, just where it should have been all the time. Three steamers sighted.

Sailed up the Bay and sighted Nantasket shore at four in the afternoon. A good, steady breeze but dusky. Can't find that shirt ribbon, the white one, to make a bow for my hat. The foggy fates have conspired to make me get a new one. Or was it a sacrifice they took to clear the fog away? Am I going batty, too?

Monday, SEPTEMBER 18, 1911. (Boston, would you believe it?)

Anchored off Baker's Island last night. Sailed in early this A.M. Hired a launch to set me ashore from the stream and spent all day in Boston. Returned on board by launch in the early evening just as the tug was docking the *Hopkins.* Shopped furiously all along Washington Street and up at Houghton's. We're going to Maine, so must get busy on my new suit. Shall never forget the last time in Thomaston when the ladies gave me the party. I asked Fred what to wear. He said call the hostess, cousin Thankful, and ask. I did. She

said, "Oh, just anything." I was suspicious but helpless until
Central, the telephone operator, who waited for Thankful to hang
up, said, "Cousin Dorothea, I want you to know, so's you won't feel
odd, that every one of those girls are going to be all dressed up in
their best bib and tucker."

Wednesday, SEPTEMBER 20, 1911

Thirty years old today. My villainous but darling boy gave me a
present of twenty-five dollars. Wasn't that lovely after I had spent
so much money in Boston?

Took the steamer to Belfast and back down to Rockland. Up
early to cross the Rockland wharf and catch the little white steamer
Monhegan, one of Captain Archibald's, for Port Clyde. Sailed out
around impressive, high Owl's Head and down the Muscle Ridge
Channel past the picturesque fish weirs off Ash Point. Saw seven
schooners waiting for paving-block cargoes in Long Cove. Tenants
Harbor was loaded with two masters. Then on around Mosquito
Island we raced, and off Marshall's Point where suddenly opened up
the charming village of Port Clyde. How dreadful to call it Herring
Gut! No wonder Mother B. was instrumental in having it named
Port Clyde. She also got Horse Point Road changed to Pleasant
Street, she says, but apparently that change did not stick. Cousin
Alice Balano Davidson dropped in on us from Tenants Harbor, and
it was good to see her. She was so kind to us at her home in Melrose
where we were married. Her father, Captain John Balano, was lost at
sea. Fred says he never wanted to go deep-water but had set his
course for being a barge skipper on the Gowanus Canal in Brooklyn,
where he could have a daily paper and fresh milk.

From the big house at Port Clyde we took Captain J.W.'s big
Regal car, and Fred tacked along the dirt road to Martinsville, past
Aunt Phronie's house to visit Captain Joel Hupper and his lovely
wife, Aunt Mary, Roscoe's mother. Fred gave her a bottle of Madeira
wine but, much to his dismay, she said they had no use for such
anymore. The Regal had only one flat tire during the ride, which

Fred says is something, of a record. The autumn foliage, reds, yellows, and siennas all took the curse off Fred's curses at the tire. A boy stopped his trudging along the road to help Fred, and we gave him a ride, his first in an automobile, he said, to Tenants Harbor. Fred and he talked of preferring horses. Said Fred, "Up where you come from there's no autos yet, is there?" Later, I asked Fred how he knew that the boy was from up-country. "Red cap and hunting boots," said Fred. "Real swamp maniac. Our coastal boys wear rubber sea-boots, even playing ball, and sometimes go to bed in them."

Thursday, SEPTEMBER 21, 1911. (At Port Clyde, nee Herring Gut.)

Beautiful sunny day and a lovely long ride following the coves and wooded points with scads of bayberries, thick green mosses, and, here and there, the delightfully pungent smell of cute, friendly little skunk, which I love, much to the rollicking laughter of my best beau, who says I'm the first to say such a thing. "You're so god-damned different there's no wonder I love you," says he. I say amen, with reservations chalked up against our next sea-going battle. Rio is a long trip.

Friday, SEPTEMBER 22, 1911

The wind went out to the eastward and there's rain, of course, right in from the Gulf Stream.

Finally induced Mother B. to venture a ride in the Regal. Drove through mud and small ponds in the road to Martinsville to see her sister Sophronia, Aunt Phronie, who wanted to go as a nurse to the Civil War but was caught young by Captain McIntyre, one of the many boys Fred's grandfather, Captain John Hupper, rescued from the British navy and brought home to Maine to man the Hupper fleet of sailing vessels. Visited Uncle Joel and Aunt Mary, whose

daughter Marjorie is finishing up at Hebron in preparation for
Mount Holyoke. Stopped on the way back to Herring Gut (I love
that name, it fits so much better than austere Port Clyde, which is
dour Scottish and not Elizabethan, as is the majority of the raucous,
smiling village!) at Mrs. Moody's whom I persuaded to make a jacket
for me.

From the top of hill above the Balano estate of many tenements
for the clam- and sardine-factory workers one sees the noble
windmill Captain J.W. installed to supply the typhoid-ridden village
with pure water, and, far off, ranging from Mosquito Island to
Monhegan, there are hundreds of sails at any time of day; two- and
three-mast lime coasters and wood-carrying schooners and pinkies,
all beholden to the extensive limerock business of Thomaston,
Rockland, and Rockport. Then there are scores of busy vessels
plying to Long Cove for granite paving blocks to convert the
waterfront roads of Boston, New York, and Philadelphia from mud
to decent footing for the dray horses of those cities. Below the hill
and beyond the Baptist chapel, conservative brown, of course, and
the Advent church nestled in the loft of George Brown's store, one
sees the fishing fleet of white and sleekly lovely sloops off the Cold
Storage, to which Gloucester and Lunenberg salt-bankers come
daily for mackerel bait and enormous cakes of ice, which boys
push across the Fish Cove on high ramps for ten cents an hour.
Above the Fish Wharf, where two- and three-mast schooners lie
abuilding, stands Fred's ancestral home on a high point overlooking
the entrance to the harbor and, beyond, historical Monhegan, the
cradle of New England, where Breton and Cornish fishermen were
said to have salted their cod and dried their nets at least three
centuries before Columbus was born. Hupper's Island helps form
the entrance to the heavenly Gut, and that is where Captain John
Hupper, Fred's grandfather, settled, owning the whole island,
Indian gardens, trees, and rich shores, and from there sending forth
scores of vessels, captained by his sons and sons-in-law, to the West
Indies, South America, Africa, and Europe, for gold and glory.
What a glorious place is my new home; how distant the hot and cold,
gopher-ridden prairies of my father's homestead, where the only
asset is loneliness, called freedom. Go east, young gal.

Saturday, SEPTEMBER 23, 1911

An evening of pastel oranges and pinks, such as I saw today inside a sea shell. Went this morning to Thomaston by auto and took the trolley to Rockland, bouncing merrily. Such a dinner at the hospitable Thorndike Hotel, and then mouthed and rolled around on the tongue delicious pistachio ices at Mrs. Thurlow's parlor. Fuller, Cobb and Davis have a department store better than the best in Boston. Fred introduced me to rare dishes; cod tongues and sounds and cheeks are delicacies indeed, and the finnan haddie was swimming yesterday before smoked under a hogshead and over alder fire and smoke. Such a wealth these coastal people have and yet cry poverty all day. Is their penuriousness but a constant reminder to save their many blessings? One can't starve here if he can amble to the shore, as the Indians knew when they'd come to the coast each spring from up the Penobscot to feast on lobsters and cunners and clams, all caught by merely wading into the eel grass. Cousin Frank Trussell, who owns nearly as much of the village as Captain J.W., including the wharf, part of the Cold Storage, the general store, the post office, and shares in God knows how many Balano and Hupper and Fish vessels, collects twenty-five cents for cashing the check of a poor cannery worker, eats crackers and milk for supper, and won't have an auto because he says he needs the horse manure for his gardens. It is reported that when Captain J.W. came home from the *Margaret Thomas* for his annual blueberry spree, Frank looked mournfully at the bunch of bananas hanging in his store and allowed as how he loved bananas but couldn't eat them because they were too dear. Captain J.W. bought him the bunch. The next Sunday, Frank, deacon of the Baptist Chapel, where seven of the twelve stained windows tell of men lost at sea, one of them John Balano, prayed for the lax and spendthrift soul of Captain J.W.

Forgot to note that when the auto left the new state road below Thomaston, we got stuck in the mud near Gilchrist Hill and were rescued by a team of white horses pulling us to terra firma.

Called on grandmother Sarah Wall Balano, who again asked, "Be you from here or be you from away?" Went motoring without veil or coat in this lovely Indian summer weather and saw the fog creep in from the Gulf Stream where it meets the Labrador Current just offshore a bit. Such a busy, lovely day in this quaint and sparkling village, which is much more charming than any inland town. And the lingo! The accents! Orts for garbage, direct from Saxon. "Git ye beaft," said Grandma Sarah to her son, thus telling him to stay behind her. "Bindinah" sounds Asiatic but really means, "Have you been to dinner?" "Gitcha chot, come to the flhot, 'n bud the bhot," is, of course, get your coat, come to the float, and board the boat. What else could it be? Best of all the nicknames: Dump Monaghan, Spider Simmons, Crow Morris, all descriptive of the bearers. Dump is short and squat, Spider plays ball as though he had eight arms, Crow screams when talking, even whispering. "My guts is rising and fallin' with the tide" means the eating of too many clams. "Deaf as a haddock; the dogfish come with the summer complaints; I almost doubt it:" those are some of the descriptive gems heard daily.

Sunday, SEPTEMBER 24, 1911

Went to church on the Ridge, where all the tribe is buried in the "yard," even though many of their bodies are still at sea. One monument marks a Balano with the engraved message that his remains are on Tybee Island off Savannah. Another states that a Hupper was lost at sea. I'd like to add the statement, "Never found after he foundered." No wonder English is hard to teach!

"Meeting" at the Port Clyde Baptist church. Frank Trussel lead the confessions of low sin after having done nothing more evil all week than tell his wife to "hark." Had milk and pilot bread for supper, because it's sinful to gorge on the sabbath, meaning that good Calvinists should be sparing. Did you know, my daughter, before you looked it up, that the word spare comes from the Saxon "sparr," to save? It pays to serve Jesus!

Monday, SEPTEMBER 25, 1911

Hemmed my suit skirt in the dense fog and mended my red gown. My boy is out, renewing old acquaintances and telling them lies, no doubt, of the big world about which they care nothing. Most of them have seen it anyway. But few of them know where they were, beyond remembering the docks and the waterfront ginmills. Cousin Watson, the family no-good, went to sea with his older brother, Captain J.W., until set ashore off the entrance to Chesapeake Bay in the pilot boat for having insulted Mother B., has been to Rio, pronounced Rye-oh, to Cuba, spoken of as Cubee, and I couldn't make him understand that he had been to Cienfuegos until I spelt it, and he said, "o' course, Signphugos!" He might as well have stayed back home with his lobsterpots. Mother B. is bright and smart and jolly. She was the favorite of her father's ten children, the tom-boy who would help him launch vessels, and she can still row a boat so well that she made Fred give her the oars to the dory yesterday when he was setting her on the island to visit her brother Orrin. Still she wouldn't eat the famous strawberries in Rio in December, because at home they were out of season, and she still can't understand why sailing south from the equator isn't easier than sailing the other way because it's downhill all the way. I do believe, though, that she's joshing me, and I'd better be a bit less proud of my brilliance in the company of these people, who like to act ignorant when they really are quite adept, in their own way, at things that matter to them.

Drove up the old road through Turkey to Glenmere in the enchanting autumn woods, and in came the river at several delightful coves.

Tuesday, SEPTEMBER 26, 1911

Rained all night and that settled the fog, but the roads are quagmires, so baked a cake to go with the jar of pear pickles given us

by Captain Stanton's wife en route to being fitted at Alice Moody's
for my new jacket and lovely mauve belt, which shows that my
shipboard fare has added an inch or two to my buxom belly. As we're
probably bound for Rio, I shan't worry about my girth. The Latins
love plump women. If Fred wants a sylph, I'll tell him that only
Parisians like slender girls and that I'll gladly starve if he'll get us a
charter to France.

Wednesday, SEPTEMBER 27, 1911

Union Fair! and the "trick the man done." Hundreds of sunburned
mouths from all the gaping. Fifty-four miles in the machine and only
two flat tires. Wonderful Camden Hills in the distance, the hills
which marked fishing grounds for the Europeans since the
Icelanders sailed and rowed along the coast nine-hundred years ago
and told no one, especially not the Pope, since all good fishermen
don't want their best spots visited by anyone. And the Pope was
Spanish, too, and wanted his people to catch the bacalao. Can you
blame Henry the Eighth for telling him to cut bait?

Stopped at the Washburn mansion in dear old Thomaston.
They've built the family's vessels at Port Clyde and Thomaston for
years. Started as sailmakers for the big square-riggers built for the
Baring Brothers Bank of London back when Yankee ships sailed the
British under and the smart bankers knew where to go for the best.

The road lined with trees loaded with luscious red apples and
green firs above the gem of a winding river. But to get information
about these things that interest my prying mind is enough to make
me nearly burst with frustration. These downeasters act so stolidly
when asked for names and explanations. But oh how they exude
over an anecdote belittling someone or over a meal of clam chowder,
lobster, blueberry pie with ice cream. And the descriptions: "That
alewife was well-timbered."

Friday, SEPTEMBER 29, 1911

Two days of visiting. The Waterman's at Ash Point, from California
where they made a fortune after being carried there free by Captain

John Hupper around the Horn, to get rid of them, Fred says. Fred sailed the car to call on them and on the Skinners and Captain Joel Hupper. With all his landroving, I am getting sea fever, so, after the lobster dinner coming up, I'll start hemming my Rio Dress. I shall also read up on Brazil and find some Cape Cod "bravo" to mimic for the Portuguese accent, which is much softer than Spanish. With all that done, the trip to Rio will materialize or else I shall throw to Neptune not only my old shoes but also that old pink gown I've been wearing for years, just because it hasn't the grace to quit and get tattered. Neptune can use it for one of his mermaids, the old philanderer.

Tuesday, OCTOBER 31, 1911. (Boston)

Sailing tomorrow for Rio. I've had such a sea fever since my last entry, weeks ago, that I just couldn't burden you, my poor diary, with such stuff as who baked what apple pie. Maine was exquisitely beautiful, and the people so warm and kind; but it's not Rio de Janeiro. It's more jolly to have Fred tacking the ship instead of the auto, rain doesn't seem strange at sea as it does on land, food tastes better, even the lobsters we brought with us on board. Good-bye to great Aunt Katie Seavey, who, having been a sea widow for fifty-seven years, will hardly miss us. Farewell to Aunt Phronie and her misbegotten Civil War as well as to Grandmother Sarah, who still doesn't know whether I'm "from here or from away." Adios to Mother B., who showed me the island where she roved and ranged along the shore, picking lobsters out of the eel grass, Indian trinkets from the old Indian garden, and spent her girlhood as a better sailor and fisher than her sea-going brothers, and came "ashore" as soon, no sooner, as she was betrothed to Captain J.W., who was smart enough to marry the owner's daughter. *Au revoir* to the Pinkhams and to Mary Davis, who jumped from the frying pan of teaching in Puerto Rico to marrying a lobster fisherman at Port Clyde, a situation not to be described so much as a leap into a fire as into a cold douche. *Aufweidersehn* to naughty cousin Perce and his proclivities for raunchy stories and raunchier women, whose nastier aspects he held up before Fred to try undermining the holy knot, which no man should rip asunder, damn him. Short shrift to the damnable auto, which caught fire one morning and had a collision the same afternoon. Even an impatient shrug to the Columbus Day procession, and I used to love parades. Miles of Italians marching past the Governor's pavillion and sixteen other lands represented with gaudy banners and silly streamers as I clung with boredom to an iron fence and longed for the open sea and its perfume of good salt, some of which the marchers should have used for a bath. I may miss the Keith Theatre, but not until I'm at sea awhile, because the tumbling, dancing, singing, and joking was good, but it might be more appreciated after a long passage at sea, which I now look forward to so long as my skipper, in his skipping, doesn't get his feet caught too often in his mouth. Shall really miss Tremont Temple and its splendid male quartet, with Dr. Cortland giving practicable prayers instead of sky-piloting. Shall miss, too, those splendid paintings by Sargent in the Public Library, the Law and the Prophets, Moses in bas-relief. Can take with me fond memories of Lulu Glaser, who played a charming and distinguished lead in Miss Didelsack; and the opera and the Boston Theater's ghost dance of chorus girls; and new Old South Church, Reverend Gordon; and the magic at the Mechanics Exposition, where the United Shoe Machinery Company's booth showed new methods of manufacturing. Lovely Aida, my favorite opera, I'll take with me to sea, because I can't stop humming L'Estudiantina. I shall ever thank Mrs. Hopkins, the wife of the man for whom the vessel was named, for presenting me with *The Winning of Barbara Worth* and *Two Years Before the Mast* as a going-away gift. Too, I shall have with me at sea memories of Blanche Bates's wonderful acting in *Nobody's Widow* at the Hollis. She's a powerful actress.

Wednesday, NOVEMBER 1, 1911. (Boston)

Loaded at last and bound for Rio with the usual Christmas cargo which Fred and his father have carried to Rio for years: ice, packed in sawdust, and topped off with barrels of apples. Away we go!

NOON. Away we did *not* go! Not enough wind to fly a kite and the fog so thick one can't see the jibboom. Towed out to a humiliating anchorage on the East Boston flats. Fred and I shared our misery by visiting Captain and Mrs. Hinckley on board the *Harwood Palmer*. Later, Captain Jim Creighton of Thomaston visited us and said there would be a chance to get to sea in the morning. He claimed the wind would go around nor'west because his leg had stopped aching. He saw our chicken coop atop the deckhouse and advised me to stuff my ears with cotton each night. "Otherwise that rooster'll ruin your beauty sleep," he said.

P.M. Finished reading *The Winning of Barbara Worth* and started *Two Years Before The Mast*, which Fred says is fiction. It doesn't read like fiction. Fred kept interrupting with talk about buying a farm.

Thursday, NOVEMBER 2, 1911. (4 A.M.)

Rushed into a few clothes and scurried on deck, awakened by the creaking rigging. The mizzen sail majestically lifted in the gray darkness to the sound of rough voices. Then appeared the main and foresails. The great booms swung into position. Next the stately great spanker and, as if staged, a great red ball of sun. Below the fort we hoisted forestaysail and outer jib. Flying jib still tied up.

Sailing out of bay all day in company with many schooners and steamers. Passed Cape Cod Light at sunset. Put a whole basket of clothes to soak. Fred spent most of the evening buying a farm — the last thing I, brought up on a farm, want to hear about. I'll take *Two Years Before The Mast*. Fred says he's going to have the crew build a gangway so I won't have to use the ladder. Told him that was very thoughtful of him. I want a child and he presents me with a gangway!

Friday, NOVEMBER 3, 1911. (At Sea.)

Will I ever get those clothes washed? Not if I continue to sleep mornings. Better let the rooster wake me. . . . Nor'west snow flurries. A large Cunarder passed, bound for wonderful Europe.

Saturday, NOVEMBER 4, 1911.

Clothes finally dried. Sewed on ship flags. Such good apples. Off we go on a course towards the Cape Verde Islands to make our easting and catch the northeast trades for the slant to Rio. A stiff westerly is scudding us along at a good rate. Made cornstarch ice cream. There's plenty of ice!

Monday, NOVEMBER 6, 1911

Rough and tumbly sea. Finished a pillow slip. Tired. Vessel too jumpy to do much sewing. At least it's a good excuse to read.

Wednesday, NOVEMBER 8, 1911. (55°15′ West Longitude, 37°25′ North Latitude.)

In center of stormy region of Gulf Stream. Wind southerly and blowing like fury. All sails on but outer jib and two topsails; Fred carries sail when others would take them in. Embroidered on nightgown. Fred shook out reef in spanker this morning. Is it to make work? He claims it's a sin for a crewman not to be busy. Will I ever get the starching and ironing done? Ought to wash my hair. I took the sights today, and Fred said I was within a heaving-line's distance of his position.

Saturday, NOVEMBER 11, 1911

Awful sea running and a sou'west gale blowing. All sails down and tied up. Only the rudder to steer by. Lying in trough of sea. The cabin furniture danced merrily about until the steward tackled piece by piece and moored them.

Sunday, NOVEMBER 12, 1911

No ice cream today. Main boom gone overboard and mizzen sail followed it, flying. Mountainous seas running all day. No chance for sights. Hoisted storm trysail. Crew bent new mizzen. All hands got soaked.

Monday, NOVEMBER 13, 1911. (44°34′ West Longitude, 34°04′ North Latitude.)

Storm trysail parted in center at midnight. No sails on until morning. Finished embroidering my new initials on nightgown and will wear it to show Fred tonight.

Tuesday, NOVEMBER 14, 1911

Wind northerly. All sails set except main, topsails, and outer jib. Wind shifty and sea so treacherous that we tried oil to calm it. The oil helped. My boy is tired. Sights at 8:45, and I worked mine out almost as quickly as did Fred. He must be tired!

Wednesday, NOVEMBER 15, 1911. (43°22′ West Longitude, 32°20′ North Latitude.)

Fished main boom. All sails set at last. Ironed. Served on [reinforced] flags. Put up a new curtain in the closet, and Fred said, "No wonder you got through the University of Minnesota on wind and no cash, if you can make a nice curtain out of scrap sails."

Started on a set of doilies for Mother B's Christmas present.

Thursday, NOVEMBER 16, 1911

All sails set but no wind. Fred says it reminds him of a former teammate on the Port Clyde baseball team who was "all windup and no pitch."

Rain squall in P.M. Back almost broken from ironing. Still have fresh vegetables. Must buy a book on astronomy to study stars. How shall I ever get through this long trip? I know! I'll make ice cream. Fred says that way out here in the middle of the Atlantic my ice cream tastes as good as Mrs. Thurlow's in Rockland. A compliment? With these downeasters it's hard to tell.

Friday, NOVEMBER 17, 1911. (39°58′ West Longitude, 31°45′ North Latitude.)

Houghton, 2nd mate, logged for incompetence and demoted to sailor. Am bored to extinction. Little wind. Made fudge.

P.M. Wind rising. Saw several schools of flying fish. Resumed *Two Years Before The Mast*. Very interesting and real. Only thirteen out of twenty-two chickens left. The others all drowned in the gale.

Saturday, NOVEMBER 18, 1911. (36°00′ West Longitude, 30°32′ North Latitude.)

Dawson now standing in as second mate but prefers to stay in forecastle with the other three blacks, all good sailors. Houghton standing watches as sailor but allowed to keep his room aft. Sold a good bit of soap to the crew tonight.

Sunday, NOVEMBER 19, 1911

Flying fish on board, but died before I could get him back in the water. Wind sou'west, and we're making great speed with all sails set. Sailors' wash out on lines up forward. Made fudge today, and Fred ate most of it. Will he ever stop eating? Chicken for dinner. Will we get the northeast trades in a few days? Then we'll come about for Rio. I doubt that Fred ever read one page of *Two Years Before The Mast*. It was written by no landsman.

Monday, NOVEMBER 20, 1911. (29° 00′ North Latitude, 34° 35′ West Longitude.)

Wind came around to northeast. Hurray! A fine, fair wind just where we want it. Says Fred: "Shows what poor luck and bad management will do." Says I: "Your management or God's?" Says Fred: "He and I work together."

Fred painting closet in chart room with right hand and eating fudge with left. I finished sewing on my linen gown in deck chair. To take fuller advantage of the beautiful breeze we rigged a spare jib between the fore and main and another between the main and mizzen. Fred says soon the vessel will be all top and no bottom. Trolling for dolphin with a long line over the stern.

The sun sank gloriously into a white bank of fog on the horizon, lighting the water to deep purple while to windward the sky is the same dull gray above bluest of waters. Peace disturbed by a yell from Fred as the troll line went taut. He bounded to the rail, barefooted, and in what looked like one leap. Fresh fish tomorrow!

Tuesday, NOVEMBER 21, 1911. (21° 18′ North Latitude, 32° 20′ West Longitude. Course: S. by E.)

N.E. wind continues fine and fair. Sailors painting house. I started more Christmas presents. Beautiful sunset. Fred must have eaten enough dolphin to make him sick.

Wednesday, NOVEMBER 22, 1911. (Cloudy; no sights.)

Neither of the Balanos feels well today. The fish? Or the pork scraps? Sails on starboard side now for six days. Fred says he'd like to shift them to the other side but would lose distance by changing course for even a few hours.

Thursday, NOVEMBER 23, 1911

Washed! Washed! Awful!

Friday, NOVEMBER 24, 1911. (17°01′ North Latitude, 27°40′ West Longitude.)

About one degree due west of the Cape Verde Islands; course, due south. Ironed and ironed. Very unhappy in this beautiful weather. Is it because Fred says we shall have no baby until we get a farm?

Saturday, NOVEMBER 25, 1911

Sighted three steamers bound northeast. Much phosphorescence on the water last night. Easterly winds this morning. A fourth steamer, the *Argyll of Newcastle*, came close to us, and we signaled her to report us. Caught another dolphin. We'll try it without pork scraps even though it breaks the old steward's heart.

Sunday, NOVEMBER 26, 1911. (11°03′ North Latitude, 25°06′ West Longitude.)

Schools of porpoises playing all day about vessel, and flying fish very beautiful. Made cornstarch ice cream. Bilge pump shows surprisingly little melting of ice cargo.

Monday, NOVEMBER 27, 1911. (8°25′ North Latitude.)

In the doldrums, and it squalled early this morning; so no longitude sight. I now understand why Fred promoted Dawson. As Fred says, Dawson would be a captain if he were white. During the squall the ability of the man showed. The sequence:

"Cap'n, cap'n," with a knock on the port.

"Yes, Dawsie?"

"Cap'n, dere am a little white squall ahead."

"Take in the outer jib."

"Dey's a doin' it now, suh."

A bit later:

"Cap'n, dat white squall am gettin' big and black."

"Take in the topsails, Dawsie."

"Dey's done got it done, suh."

Will we ever get to Rio? Stole another barrel of apples today.

Wednesday, NOVEMBER 29, 1911. (5°30′ North Latitude.)

Washed! Made only one degree since yesterday noon. At this rate, Christmas will get to Rio before we do. Poor Rio, without Christmas ice. Poor me, with the gangway coming nicely instead of a baby.

Thursday, NOVEMBER 30, 1911

Thanksgiving for most people but not for me. Last night, in the deck chairs with the Great Dipper close, talked to Fred about a baby. First he said that he was enough for me to handle right now. Then he said we'd get a farm first. That got him on farming, about which he knows nothing beyond the fact that he likes the taste of vegetables. Ironed all day until my back felt broken.

Saturday, DECEMBER 2, 1911

Passed a European bark last night bound for that delectable land. A farm indeed! Not for little me. Still calm but very rough; there's been quite a blow somewhere near us. Shifted sails to port side for the first time in two weeks. Still four degrees north of equator. Steamer passed on weather bow, bound for Africa. Head winds for us. Lucky steamer. Rio is so far away. Shall take the curse off by making ice cream.

Sunday, DECEMBER 3, 1911

Made cornstarch ice cream with a can of strawberries in it. Feeling blue. Fred said, "What can I do to show my great love?" I said: "Have some more ice cream." What I did not say was, "Stop farming and let me start a baby."

Monday, DECEMBER 4, 1911

 Full moon calm. I am bored. Is it the farm or the moon? Passed a steamer this morning and sighted a squarerigger. No sleep last night after the day's washing and am all in today. Feel as though I'd been on a week's spree. Fred says I look it.

   Hot, hotter, hottest! Seventy-three miles north of the line and a little east of Saint Paul's Rocks. Two thousand miles to Rio.

Thursday, DECEMBER 7, 1911. (3°20′ South Latitude, 28°00′ West Longitude.)

In bed the past two days with pains. Never a child for me, I guess. Going blind with reading and sewing. God send us Rio before I lose both sight and mind. Fred fishing and I consoling myself with thoughts of the gangway. Some consolation!

Sails still on port side. Fine trade winds. Crossing the line, Fred tried to cheer me up with the story about the woman tourist who asked the steamer captain to point out to her the equator. The old devil plucked a hair from his head and put it across his binoculars so the woman could see the "line". She was most pleased and then asked, "And is that a camel walking on the line?"

That new jibboom guy has been troubling Fred a good bit.

Saturday, DECEMBER 9, 1911. (32°03' West Longitude, 8°34' South Latitude.)

Wind died out during P.M. Made salad for supper to keep my mind off gangways, moons, dolphins, and Fred. Little does a woman know of her husband when she marries, but she learns quite soon. I suppose I should be thankful that I can go to sea with him. It could be worse; say on a farm, for instance. Selah!

Sunday, DECEMBER 10, 1911. (10°30' South Latitude, 33°00' West Longitude.)

Another dolphin! Fred says we carry our own fresh-fish market along with us. Steamer sighted last night, bound north. Husband shown my plans for a house. Not for five years, he said, and then one with furnace, fireplaces, and a bath. Great! But must I wait five years for a home and children? Not on your tintype!

Monday, DECEMBER 11, 1911. (13°18' South Latitude.)

Served another pair of linen drawers. Fred painted after companionway. Doesn't our gangway look splendid! Sails still on starboard side. Fred says they must be aching.

Tuesday, DECEMBER 12, 1911. (15°39′ South Latitude. 840 miles to Rio.)

Men doused awning with salt water to prevent mold. Aired the linen locker. My old white Peter Pan blouse is wearing out, thanks be. From looking over log books of past voyages I find that we may be becalmed in this spot for a week or more. So much for Fred's usual statement that God Almighty's wind is stronger than steam.

Wednesday, DECEMBER, 13, 1911

Calm all day. In company with full-rigged Norwegian ship.

Heigh-ho! Isn't it awful to have to wash every week? But the tropics take so many clothes, and I cannot bear smelly ones. Tomorrow is washday. Served mattress cover. Only 540 miles to Rio! Will we ever get there? Can't possibly make it before Monday at best and will lose our premium of $100 per day for each day under forty-five days for the total trip.

Thursday, DECEMBER 14, 1911. (19°20′ South Latitude, 36°00′ West Longitude.)

Fred has been fun today and even helped me with the wash.

Ex-Second Mate Houghton is tarring down the rigging in the bosun's chair. Dawson is lowering him away. Such is justice on the good ship *Hopkins!*

Beautiful flaky little clouds in a brilliant blue sky. Clothesline parted and new skirts and blouses all spotted. Wish we were in Rio, going places. Is it my farm background that makes me want to go places and see everything.?

Friday, DECEMBER 15, 1911

Wore ship. Sails on port side nearly a month except for short times. Fred said he could hear the booms groaning with toothaches so he had to shift them.

P.M. Sails back to port to hold course. Amen!

While Houghton was aloft we dug out his room and for once the door is open. Poor little half man. All seafaring men, even to skippers, are very pronounced characters with strong peculiarities. Houghton is to be paid off in Rio if we ever get there.

Saturday, DECEMBER 16, 1911. (240 miles to go to Cape Frio.)

Good breeze blew up from nor'west. We boomed along all night and all day. Stamped Mother B's doilies. Taking an inventory of everything for entering the ship at customs in Rio. Made fudge; first time I've felt like it in weeks. If that villainous husband of mine ever tells me how much better is Helen G's fudge than mine again, I'll throw the entire mess overboard.

Sunday, DECEMBER 17, 1911

N.W. wind all night. Fred up early looking for land. Cape Frio rumored to be some forty miles to westward. Dawson climbed spanker rigging to look for it. Much fog. No land at 8 A.M.

9 A.M. Land ho! Feel like Columbus making San Salvador and Balboa beholding the gentle Pacific. Those two can't hold a candle to my joys at seeing the mountains of Brazil, the fingers of God, they're called. Chocolate ice cream today.

Monday, DECEMBER 18, 1911

Becalmed between Cape Frio and Rio. Wouldn't you know! Is it the
Sugar Loaf we see so tantalizingly in the distance? Is it hot!

Tugboat at 1:30 P.M. A big engine in a small white hull. One
man clad in tattered white drawers and a long knife hailed us in
English, fluent but hardly understandable. Forty pounds sterling to
tow us in and, later, out. Fred talked him down to thirty while I
fumed over downeast niggardliness. What's ten pounds between us
and Rio? My lovely, varnished gangway over the side and a new
awning up for entertaining friends. My spirits are soaring.

Sugar Loaf, a stupendous rock, upended. Wonderful line of
dotted beach for miles and miles and electric lights along the
diamond necklace of Botafogo Bay. The forts fired salutes to us as
we entered entrancing Rio. Much mail, many beautiful tall ships
and, on the dock, many friends, including Otis Fales from
Thomaston. Hundreds of Brazilians waiting for the ice. It should be
a Merry Christmas.

Wednesday, DECEMBER 20, 1911. (Rollicking Rio)

Sea fever will come slow and hard in this wondrous city. Even the
several German men-of-war anchored in the glittering bay cannot
detract from the beauty of the hilled, colorful, pink-and-white
paradise. Guanabara, the name for the bay, is native Indian for
"breast of the sea." It availed little that they kept their minds above
their belts, but then, according to the old photos, they wore no belts
or anything else. Nor would I wear anything in this sultry climate if
I could put up with a bit of rape. Clothes are against the spirit of the
place. No wonder the Jesuit missionaries wrote that they could
discover no virgin younger then ten years of age. South of here,
from Porto Alegre (Happy Port) down to Paraguay, the soldiers of
the cross ran a theocratic dictatorship in the seventeen hundreds,

not too different from that of the Puritans about Boston at the same time. Above here one sees the "Dedos de Deus," the fingers of God, rising to the heavens in mountainous peaks near Petropolis, where the Emperor, Dom Pedro II, summered and where every Carioca worth his salt scoots annually for a summer chill. Yellow fever was then almost as epidemic in lovely Rio as now. We were told yesterday that several of the Norwegian barks and English steamers in the harbor have had as many as two whole crews shipped out from Europe to replace those who have died of the yellow jack. Were also told of the typical Brazilian, his brain and that of his passing cousin hot with the torpid heat, who bumped into his cousin in one of the narrow sidewalks of the city and, after trying to remember who each other was, decided with great effort to make conversation, as follows:

"Oh, cousin Aristodemo, it is really you. And how is your beautiful mother, my beloved aunt, I think?"

"Yes, your aunt. Actually she is dead."

A long pause while Aristodemo's mind wrestles slowly with how to show grief and his cousin copes with the rumor of bad news, already fleeing from his consciousness.

"Dead? Of what?"

"Yellow fever, it might have been."

Another pause for futile attempt to regain a foggy consciousness; then a valiant effort to carry on and finish the onerous conversation: "Yellow fever. Hmnn. Ay! Yellow, what a beautiful color!"

The *Marie* and the *Hopkins* are the only ships in the harbor flying the American flag, the peppermint candy rag, as the British call it, and both ships are from Maine.

The white steam launches to Niteroi across the bay scoot as quick and thick as water bugs on a pond. The *mercado*, where they disgorge multitudes of laughing, dancing, noisy cargoes of plump girls and musical boys with the ability to make a symphonic orchestra out of spoons, sticks, and rubber bands on match boxes, is loaded with enormous avocados at a penny each, luscious pineapples, and juicy mangoes, which wet your chin and stain your dress, but who cares. Just in from the lazy, smelly waterfront, the bay curves on both sides like a horseshoe off south past Botafogo to the Sugar Loaf and north to Governor's Island and the sun-baked forts where soldiers siesta on duty.

Captain Rodin, an ancient Breton pirate now settled here and reputed to own the redlight district, came on board for dinner, and, says Fred, he brings a different "wife" each trip.

It is surprising what excellent condition our ice cargo is in. The consignee, Senhor Ferrera, is very pleased with it and stayed to take a pleasant launch ride with us during the cool (the less hot) of the evening, when the diamond necklace of lights along Botafogo Bay made it seem brilliantly impossible that there should be anything like yellow fever. We went outside, around the Sugar Loaf and along the white beach of Copacabana, south to the Arpeador, the jutting rock sticking out into the sea from where fish are speared as they surface to the night lights. Does the word *arpeador* have anything to do with harpoon? Must look it up. If so, an arpeador is a harper and Harper's Ferry is no longer to me anything but a place where some Harpers settled who probably never knew that in old English — or was it Norman French? — their name derived from their occupation at harping. The English language is as much mixed up as was poor Aristodemo. Imagine the silliness of Washington in trying to teach Puerto Ricans English! At least trying to make English supplant the more simple but, of course, less rich language, Spanish. And this Portuguese, so wooshy and so full of carioca slang. "Jogo do bicho," the numbers game where every *carioca* tries to guess the beast whose picture will appear at appointed places the next day, has become a commonplace expression for a foolish endeavor. "Amigo da onza," friend of the beast, is used by all to mean an unreliable person. I love it, oh how I do love my carefree *cariocas*. They should care, for most are poor, but they don't. My lewd Fred says a Brazilian breakfast is nothing but a cigarette and a piss. Yet with my own eyes, I've seen the harbor alive with fish for the catching, shrimp can be caught along the shore with no more effort than that required to pick them up. The trees are drooping with fruit. I suppose it's sheer laziness. And how the delightful humorous *cariocas* like to joke of that. I've heard the tale twenty times in these few days of the Emperor asking reclining country *cabolco* whether his land was good for farming. The man said the land was rich. "A terra da?" asked the Emperor, "Does the land give a good yield?" "Si, Senhor," replied the peasant, "plantado, da." "If it's planted, it yields." Many *cariocas*, it is said, merely exist from one *carnaval* to another, spending the year between in mirthful misery.

That reminds me of the real world; we began to discharge cargo. The Italian stevedores (the *cariocas* won't work, so laborers have to be imported) with towels around their necks and sashes of red or yellow about their waists sing out their curses with voices of opera stars.

Captain Rodin for supper, and I was invited to tour the redlight district, heavily veiled he insisted, to see how happy and homelike are the whores, just honest, hard-working girls, he insisted. I suppose the hard-working part of it is true, their area of business being so close to sailors. In the evening, we took a launch ride and visited the palace at Laranjeras, where the Emperor used to live; cool buildings with many arches of white among the orange trees. Apparently Captain Rodin and the president of Brazil are close friends. The company I keep may not be the best, but it certainly is enlightening!

Thursday, DECEMBER 21, 1911

On shore, where we called on Dr. and Mrs. Shaw, old friends of Captain J.W. Their daughter Roxy is studying singing and has such a beautiful voice that she has been invited to Milan for further development at the Opera. Lord knows she's fat enough to be a prima donna. They invited us to Christmas dinner. Mrs. Shaw was educated at the swank girls school in Vevey, Switzerland. Not content with a little knowledge, she kicked over the conventional traces and went to the Sorbonne. What a joy to talk with someone who can read without moving her lips. She said that Captain J.W. would be very proud of me, if we ever meet, because he had told her several times how much he missed having an education. Apparently he went away to sea when he was twelve, without having gone beyond the sixth grade, but reads voraciously, as I've seen many sailors do. Caught one of the black crewmen cuddled in the lee of the forward house yesterday puzzling over a thick volume of Shakespeare. It's a good thing Fred didn't see it. He might claim that the literate sailor was up to no good.

Took the tram out to Leme. The delightful *cariocas* call their streetcars *bondes*. That's because the Electric Bond and Share Company financed the street railways, floating bonds. In typical wittiness, the *cariocas* assume that each bond bought one car, so naturally each car is a *bonde*. The reasoning behind the idea has long been forgotten but the name *bonde* sticks, just as in Puerto Rico a bus is a *gua-gua*, from the noise made by the air-filled, rubber pump for the horn.

We stopped for a demitasse of Rio coffee when we were waiting for the return *bonde* at Leme. Sugar is poured into the little white cup up to the brim, and the hot, syrupy coffee is slowly dropped into the sugar until the cup is full. Then with one gulp, all is downed. If there's any delay and an impatient American asks how long it will take to get the goo, the answer is always the same, and typically Brazilian: "Esta na maquina," it's in the works. Local businessmen find the *cafezinho*, the little coffee, an efficient way for terminating a conversation and getting rid of pests. They invite their visitor out to the corner coffee shop, each corner has one, and when the visitor is speechless with his throat afire, the businessman will slap his visitor on the back, say "Ate logo," "so-long," and disappear while his visitor is helpless.

Above Leme looms the Corcovado, the hunchback figure of natural mountain up which one climbs for a view over the bay and the sea. The new boulevard, Parisian in design but Brazilian in maintenance, with many potholes already, is lined with beautiful palms. The *bonde* returned to the Municipal Theatre stop, where I read of operas to come and there met Mrs. Fales of Thomaston. Her husband once sailed as mate with Captain J.W. She will go to the opera with me, but I could tell that she looked upon it distastefully and might prefer a "time" at the South Thomaston Grange. Captain Fales and Fred met us for another *cafezinho* and sailed ships, while I drank in the sounds of Rio and guzzled the delights of the brilliant colors of parrots on the shoulders of shouting hawkers (did hawkers once sell birds?) who were exhorting each *carioca* to add the noise of the birds to the already deafening pandamonium of the typical *carioca* home.

Friday, DECEMBER 22, 1911

The old steward won a thousand milreis, about four hundred dollars, in the lottery and is scouring Brazil for real German beer. Fred says not to expect any fudge or clean bedsheets for weeks, unless I get to work myself. Went ashore for photos and visited the waterfront market, which goes on for several blocks. Melons brought in the sloops, *goletas* from along the coast, sell for less than a dollar. Watched a big Norwegian bark being towed in among the constantly scooting ferry boats. Walked, or sauntered, along the market and saw such things as I couldn't believe: oysters picked from shoreside trees, shrimp as long as small lobsters, pineapples hollowed out to be filled with large and luscious strawberries. Reminds me of Fred's tale about the Maine boy, home from the sea, who told his old grandmother that he had seen fish that fly and she said, "Now son, I'll believe ye seen rivers of silver (Rio de la Plata) and coasts of gold (Rio d'Oro) but flying fish! Don't tell your poor old granny they's fish that fly!"

A launch ride during the cool of the evening with the Fales and their son Otis, based in Rio with Otis Elevator, and "uplifting" the Brazilians, he says, out around the Sugar Loaf and along the Copacabana, which, Fred says, his father was offered at a low price ten years ago and now is worth that sum by a hundred times. Fred says his father had refused the deal saying he had no use for all that sand, that it would ballast ships and wasn't good for anything else.

Otis's friend, Danny Danforth of Ellsworth and just out of the University of Maine, came along for the ride. He's down here drumming up business for Remington-Rand and intends to stay. Had with him a belle from the ancient English colony of Niteroi, a poetess, with whom I traded quotes all evening, much to the amazement and maybe consternation of the others. But she and I had a lovely time. We even sang the baccarol together in time with the roll of the launch in the swelling seas, just as it should be sung.

Saturday, DECEMBER 23, 1911

Dinner on shore: figs, yellow and luscious, served in thick whipped cream, a lovely *bife*, steak from the southern Rio Grande do Sul cattle ranches, tasty yams, and the rice sprinkled with shredded manioc-like tapioca. The mail steamer comes Christmas day, so we'll have a double joy. Took the Aguas tram with electric cogs up the Corcovado and marvelled at the view below. There was Tijuca off to the right, with its anvil mountain and the bar below, which stretches out into the sea and causes strong currents known as the Cemetery of the Americans, from the fact that unknowing bathers get too far out from the beach and never return. From the center view, there is Botafogo Bay to the left of Leme and far left the Fingers of God rising up to cool, pleasant Petropolis. Rio is a city of red-tiled roofs, clinging clouds to filter the strong sun. I walked down through the lovely, cool rain forest among large ferns, where lovers lingered amongst pink and purple orchids, and a solitary policeman turned his back when great advances were made. He smiled at me as though to say that he and I understood. I felt like a wood nymph, above it all.

Oh Brazil, BRAZIL, how I do love you. I love you but I'm watching you. You're tricky like champagne, but oh so warming and so enticing. The good old USA shall always come first, but you, my Brazil, have my heart, to say nothing of my stomach. You'll be my second true love, at least 'till I get to France. Fickle am I? So, too, are you, I surmise.

Then walked through old Lanjeras to the beach and waded while I dreamed of the delightful life of a beachcomber before being jolted back to sensibility by cries from Fred, something about,

"Where the hell have you been and what in hell do you think you're doin'," and "I brought these flowers for you and now they're all wilted and not worth a pisshole in the snow." Reality!

Sunday, DECEMBER 24, 1911

Market after church. Fred follows his father's showmanship of attending Catholic church to be seen there by the consignees of the cargo, who are led to believe that these descendants of Puritans, dissenters, anti-papists and such, are true believers. Well, Paris was worth a mass to Henri Quatre! And next to Paris I'll take the annual trips to Rio. Mass couldn't possibly hurt anyone, but I wonder if my ancestor Elder Brewster turned slightly in his Plymouth grave when I sprinkled holy water on my brow. After that we took Mrs. Amado for a ride in the launch. She's an old friend of Captain J.W. and runs the telephone company like father Bell, whom she knew when he and Emperor Dom Pedro set up the first telephone company. It was from Niteroi to Rio. More a toy of the Emperor's than a commercial success, it still is spoken of as the world's first. Like all of my dear Brazil, it was an unfinished symphony, but just as lovely as Schubert's, I do wish we had a gramaphone on board. I need good music. And so to bed with Schubert's Unfinished finished as I dropped off with thoughts of begging, borrowing, or pirating a record-playing machine. Dreamed I was on the Esterhazy estate with Schubert.

Sunday, DECEMBER 24, 1911. (Christmas Eve in Rio de Janeiro.)

Market this A.M. Giant avocadoes, big as volley balls and ever so tasty with vinegar and oil as we ate them sitting on the quai with our feet dangling above the fruit-laden goletas with their crews of all shades from blue-black to *cafe com leite*. Flowers galore did Fred get me to make up for the scene of yesterday, which I'd forgotten with

Schubert on my brain but which elephantine Fred did not. Read
Tennyson during the launch ride while Fred and Mrs. Amado
flirted, much to my disgust but real relief at being left alone to read
and dream and drink in the Rio, which is now part of me. Tennyson
would have written of Rio as I feel it. Fred says it's alright so long as
they pay the freight monies in pounds sterling, the only currency in
the world, except for the Austrian Maria Theresa thaler, that's hard
and here to stay forever as the world's basic money. On board found
the *New York Times*, delivered by steamer, and how odd to read of
snow and ice when we smell mangoes, their turpentine odor, and
hear the royal palms swishing in the trade winds. It can't be
Christmas Eve! Next I'll refuse strawberries in December! As in
Puerto Rico and other Iberian countries the children here do not get
presents at Christmas but on Three Kings Day, El Dia de los Tres
Reyes Magicos, when they put out straw and water the night before
for the camels of the Wisemen, go to sleep, and find their gifts in the
morning, delivered by the wise men, just as did the Christ child.
Fred says it's because Santa Claus would find it hard sledding!

Monday, DECEMBER 25, 1911

Merry Christmas, Rio, *o meu*. The best Christmas a heathen like me
ever was allowed to enjoy. The young poetess from Niteroi sailed
over in her sloop to present me with copies of original papers of
Tennyson which were given to one of her family by the great man's
relatives. I shall save them for when the doldrums catch us at sea. I
shall write about them. I shall copy them and send a copy to the
Boston Library and another copy to my alma mater. Bowdoin and
the University of Maine shall get copies.

Christmas dinner at Shaws with fresh asparagus soup, meats,
and vegetables for beginners followed by *lechon asado* for fillers and
topped off with Christmas pudding served all aflame in glowing
brandy, which also made me glow. Drank a secret toast to my
mother's efforts in the W.C.T.U. There were toasts in champagne to
all hands and the cook, with special bumpers for toasting Captain

J.W. When a toast was made in English it had to be translated into Portuguese, which required another glass full. Thanks to God there were no French or Russian or Chinese about. The rest of the day, evening, and night seem a bit vague to me. I do wonder why. Fred says I'm now such a sailor that all I need is a tattoo.

Tuesday, DECEMBER 26, 1911

Just what was needed for a hangover. Went through the Ferrera's cold storage plant. It was loaded with barrels of grapes, peaches, nuts, beer, and meats. They have seven ice-making machines but have to import ice because the demand is so great. Before they had the plant, and in the times of the colony, runners and fast horses were sent to the distant mountain peaks for snow.

Several sailing vessels and steamers arrived today. A beautiful Norwegian bark came in with ice from distant Norway, a week late for the best prices.

Wednesday, DECEMBER 27, 1911

Mutiny on board the *Sylva*. Mrs. Morrill and her son were sent over to us while Captain Morrill of Portland got the affair under control. The baby is too cute for words. How I'd love to have one like Baby John. But Fred says we have a full complement of crew right now. Then he had the nerve to go on shore and pay off Houghton. To console myself, I ironed and got a backache. To further console me, Fred came back with an enormous bunch of grapes, dripping cool. Three men sent to the hospital from the *Sylva*. Captain Morrill quelled the mutiny singlehanded. No wonder shipowners the world around seek out Maine skippers.

Spent, or rather capitalized, the evening ashore. Drove along the lovely Avenida Rio Branco past the exquisite gardens started by Dom Pedro, he with the chin of his Hapsburg mother, large and jutting, and with her Hapsburg mind also, small and preoccupied with gadgets and gardens. No wonder he lost his job. Saw the

Ministery of War, the artillery barracks, and the railway bridge, which Dom Pedro deplored as costing over two thousand milreis. It couldn't be replaced for ten times that. Had a heavenly supper of *tornedos* and tamarind ice cream with Captain and Mrs. Fales, who spent much of the evening anticipating the coming alewife run at Warren. Glory be!

Thursday, DECEMBER 28, 1911

Went on board the *Sylva* out of curiosity about the mutiny and against Fred's advice. A beautiful bark which carries over thirty sails when fully rigged. But that means she carries an enormous crew, three times as many as the efficient schooner-rigged *Hopkins*. How do they ever make a profit, paying and feeding so many? Mrs. Morrill says she was built in Bath (the ship, not Mrs. Morrill) but would not say word one about the recent unpleasantness. Captain Morrill's fists are as square as his square-rigged vessel and, from the set of his mouth and the steel of his glance, I'd guess he was a hard-driving martinet from whom escape would be highly pleasant, especially when a bulldozed sailor arrives in easy-going Rio. I got about as much news of important things from Mrs. Morrill as one would get of European affairs from the *Rockland Courier*, nothing, but, like the *Courier*, she was highly exhaustive on trivia, mainly of baby's colic and diaper rash. You'd think she went through a mutiny every day; perhaps she does, poor, frail little thing.

And so on to more edifying things such as Miss Peck who came on board for tea in the evening. Wonderful woman, writes fine essays for the Rio *Globo* and the *Diario*, in Portuguese. Climbs every mountain she can approach and, oh lordy, how she can talk. To split a lemon with her is to get a course in Brazilian history, complete with the names, builds, proclivities, and oddities of every one of the hundreds of mistresses of Dom Pedro the First; the Brazilians loved him as much as they detested and ridiculed his slow, German son who slept only with his wife — and the emphasis is on "slept," says

Miss Peck. It may be a commentary on his relationship with his Empress that instead of naming one of his orchids after her, he used her name for the first railroad, the Leopoldina, which still chugs uphill all night to Petropolis.

Saturday, DECEMBER 30, 1911

Fred bought me a diamond ring! Of course they are cheaper here than anywhere else in the world. Miss Peck says one fairly stumbles over them in the neighboring state of Minas Gerais (General Mines), where there is also untapped riches of iron, copper, and gems. So made fudge and cake for Fred and flirted unmercifully with him, like a fey schoolgirl. Suffered an all-night visit by the Fales, who were gorged on Aunt Mary's Martinsville pickles, while I ate what they passed by: enormous pineapples stuffed with the most luscious strawberries, maybe out of season in Martinsville but too tasty to be censored by any such silly thing as a calendar. How my diamond ring does sparkle and how many contretemps with Fred I can forgive for his thoughtfulness and generosity. Or is it a bribe, like the gangway, to shut me up about our baby. I shall offer a counter bribe by telling him we'll name the little boy, and of course it will be a boy, after his father. Selah!

Sunday, DECEMBER 31, 1911

How the Shaws did love my baked beans. Said they hadn't tasted the like since visiting their old home in Millinocket several years ago. Also said the Millinocket winters prepared them well for balmy Rio living. They shuddered when they mentioned Katahdin, and boasted of how high and mighty it was. How the Shaw children did whoop it up chasing about the decks and high, too high, into the rigging. I had to climb above the crosstrees to get one frightened little girl down. Fred said he enjoyed the view. The next time we have rambunctious, rigging-climbing imps on board I shall wear my black bloomers. I wonder if they're in the lazarette. I'll also need them for tennis with Miss Peck.

This is the last entry in my log for the year gone by. 1911 brought me my boy, my trip to Rio, and my diamond ring, to say nothing of my practical gangway. What will 1912 bring? Please God, only good things, such as a trip to Europe and my baby boy!

List for shopping in Jacksonville where we are bound light, and to reach same we shall wend our way through the enchanting West Indies:

> ribbon for underwear
> shoes
> gloves

List for Boston:

> seaboots
> oilskins and sou'wester
> silk dresses
> writing paper, scads of it
> frame photos
> needles
> film
> layette for baby (come hell and high water)

List for Barbados, in case we put in there, as Fred says he always does to get Yankee dollars for his freight money paid here in pounds: (Fred's estimates. Based on what he paid?)

> Half pound sterling for towels and hand linens
> Two pounds for 15 yards Manchester foulards
> One pound for silk waistes for Betty, mama, and sisters
> Half pound for light blue linen dress

NEW YEAR'S DAY, 1912

To my new diary:

> Dorothea Balano
> Hand and Pen

Try to be good
Now and then.

Wrote letters and postcards all morning to all and then some. Went ashore in the heat of the afternoon and mailed over forty pieces of mail at a cost of six milreis and eight hundred reis. The rei was once the unit of currency but so inflated it became, or rather depreciated so much, that the charming Brazilians just added two zeros, and now the unit, one milrei, is a thousand of the old but worth no more. It is said that Brazil receives so little for its coffee, timber, and gems that it can't pay for the staples it imports or for the machinery it needs. Thus, according to my sad efforts to read dull Adam Smith, the currency depreciates because imports cost too much. Dora, do think of more interesting things such as the *bonde* ride to Tijuca and the samba ditty you heard the youngster, he with music from a rubber band on a match box, sang over and over again as we passed the *Barra de Tijuca,* the beach. It went something like this:

	Inexact translation:
Na Barra de Tijuca	
A lua escondeu	The moon shyed away
O guarda bobeo	The copper turned his back
Plantei um beja nela	I planted a kiss on her
Ela quasi desmayo	And found she had the knack.

On the pleasant ride, I passed many beautiful homes nestled in the heights, the cool airs, of the mountain with its rain forest. The Ferreras' home stood out white and rose and pink. There's money in ice. Saw several modern, clean dairies as we ascended the steep, winding tracks from which screams and sparks flew. The conductor hovered around until I had paid two or three fares. But the trip was worth much more. Waded up a purring brook with my sandals around my neck to the falls and finally saw the cataract, high and narrow where it tumbles down a precipitous rock and breaks into three parts to meet again in the deep pool below. It is the source for the city's water, which enters on aquaducts fashioned after those the Romans built in Spain and Portugal. I wanted to swim, but a sign said "no" so drank glass after glass of the sweet, cool water until I was swimming inside of me. Among the banks of soft green ferns sprinkled with dainty wild orchids, as common here as they are rare and costly in New York, I lay me down to dream in the cool mountain air that I was a water nymph unmolested by satyrs like Fred, without whom my life would be as vapid as that of the silly nymph. Then reluctantly rose from my forest couch and trod back to the dusty *bonde*. All too soon was back in the city, but the ice cream was delicious, and, after all, what's so bad about Rio?

Last night the Avenida Rio Branco was aglow with festive lights of reds, oranges, yellows, and greens; long-legged mulatto girls pranced across the street, chased by lithe and smirking bucks, while in the *boites*, the nightclubs, such as the High-Life (pronounced Higgy-Lifee), the elite sported Parisian gowns and broad-brimmed hats while sipping cafezinhos and French liqueurs to further ruin the balance of payments. Romantic, slim, dainty, and dark gentlemen swarmed everywhere until daybreak when they stumbled merrily to mass. Oh Rio, my ethereal love!

A bunch of Maine men off a Norwegian bark, ninety days out from Gulfport (they must have sailed by way of China) with a cargo of case oil set us aboard the *Hopkins* much to the disgust of the bargaining bumboat men, who are better swindlers than boatsmen.

JANUARY 4, 1912. (Towing out to sea.)

As he learned from his father, Fred had a new towline saved for the surging ride out into the Atlantic combers, which have been gathering height and force since they left Africa. Paid the man in the dirty drawers, the factotum of the tugboat, thirty pounds for the tow in and out, and dear Rio was soon astern and dropping below the horizon. I hate to leave. For once I don't have sea fever. Diabolically wish the brand spanking new line parts.

The night before sailing Captain Herbert Rawding, for whom a schooner is being named, boarded us to wish farewell. He wanted to buy our launch, but Fred said it was mine, so not for sale. Fred said he would name it for me. Captain Rawding said that was very nice of

Fred, as he remembered the standing joke among the downeast maritime fraternity that Fred was once thinking of naming a launch the *After You* so that each of his girls could be told that the boat would be named "after you."

As Rio fell away, Masefield's "Seafever" came back to me most vividly and realistically and nostalgically:

> The ship was cheered, the harbor cleared
> and merrily did we drop
> below the town, below the kirk, below the lighthouse top,

or something like that.

As we tow out I look astern at my heart. Parts of it lie atop the Corcovado, the Sugar Loaf, the diamond necklace of Botafogo, and the lazy loveliness of Laranjeras Palace, to say nothing of my palate, which I think I see wandering along the waterfront market among the pineapples, strawberries, avocadoes, mangoes, and the exquisite pastel ices. I think of the last night in my adopted town, when Mrs. Amado taught me, singing it in the loveliest of voices, true but sensual, the long ballad of the Northeast, the plaintive song of the bandit, Lampeon, a hell-raiser Robin Hood, most evil but most loving, somehow an overdrawn but essential Brazilian who has the vices as well as the virtues of every one of my adopted countrymen and then some. Can I remember how it goes?

> *Ole mulher rendera, ole mulher renda,*
> *Si voce me faz a renda, eu t'ensenha namorar.*
> Hi there, mending woman, hi my sheltered dove
> If you show me how to mend dear, I'll show you how to love.

And the one she sang about the disgusted girl of the drunken country man who wasn't too bright, being told by his girl how to distinguish water from cashassa, the local dynamite:

> *Voce pense que cashash e agua.*
> *Cashassa noo e auga, noo.*
> *Cashass vem do guaranice*
> *E agua vem do riberaon*

You think cashash is water.
Cashash is not water, no.
Cashash comes from poisoned junk plants
And water comes from the river's flow.

And the night before sailing, at the Shaws, I shall never forget. Young Roxy sang Greig songs, and her little sisters and brothers hovered about her, enchanted with her lovely high, voluminous voice, so soft when she.wants it soft and always full of feeling. She sings only operas, and I am sure she'll make a great career for herself in Milan. All this followed by a cozy, dainty tea, with such lovely manners on the part of all, family, kids, servants.

And the shopping in Rio. Lovely tan linen, and so cheap, forty cents a yard.

Back to towing out. You say farewell and good luck to the two little old red iron warships anchored near the lofty and stately squarerigger in the lazy morning haze, which makes all three ships seem painted in the dim, blurred colors of the new impressionist school of Paris. Then you pass the saluting naval schoolship and the stout, quaint fortress in the harbor across from startling Sugar Loaf. In a trice of dreaming, a few hours pass and the flat-topped mountains behind the Corcovado, which you glory at when walking along the Leme boulevard, become a foggy, ethereal horizon. The tug casts off the brand spanking new hawser at Razia, and the irreligious but superstitious downeast skipper prays for wind to take us off the shore and out to the safety of the sea.

To sublimate dear Rio in my mind and to keep from shedding inner tears, I puttered about the closet and idled with my sewing basket, trying to dwell on trivia, but the closet reminds me of shopping in Rio and the sewing basket of the ballad about the mending woman. Au revoir dear Rio but not good-bye!

The offshore breeze blew up at 1:10 in the afternoon and we wore ship [Editor's note: shifted the sails to the other side with the wind astern instead of coming up into the wind as for tacking], and gratefully headed out to sea. Tasted the beautiful box of fruit given me by Mr. Ferreira. Breeze died before sunset and may have to anchor to prevent drifting back into land. The damnedest feeling!

The R. W. Hopkins in port.

BELOW Dorothea and Betty hanging wash on deck.

91

Set for a "spin" in the Balano family car.

Fred's Port Clyde home, "too dear for words".

92

Mending the
Spanker

A "younger" Cap'n Fred.

Dorothea before leaving Minnesota.

Dorothea and Fred's wedding photo.

The Fred B. Balano at a southern port.

97

ABOVE Looking anxiously for signs of home.

LEFT Dorothea at Arecibo, P.R. in 1910.

The skipper and the skipper's wife at sea and their first son, James, editor of this diary.

The skipper's wife, Dorothea, aboard the R. W. Hopkins.

Part of me wants the sea; the rest wants Rio. What a glorious dilemma!

JANUARY 5, 1912. (At sea.)

Breeze sprang up with the dawn airs coming off the heat of the land, and we did not have to anchor to hold our ground. Making a good deal to the southward to get sea room for rounding the jutting Cape Frio, beyond which it is straight sailing along the coast past Bahia, Recife, and on to Barbados.

Says I to Fred, "No ballast?"

Says Fred: "These are kindly seas. And ballast costs too much down here."

"But won't we turn turtle in a sudden breeze, if we're caught unwary?"

"We won't be caught."

Says I: "But we wasted days taking on ballast in the Chesapeake for the short run down to Jacksonville."

"That was hurricane season."

Says I, "Oh," innocent but still doubting.

Mainsail lowered so the gaff can be used for hoisting the sawdust, which kept the ice from melting, out of the hold to be thrown overboard. Watch below working as well, and cursing. Rio faded from sight, but not from mind. Cape Frio looms faintly in the distance, like a rumor one feels will become real, like my enchanting diamond ring, at which I stare and which I turn and fondle every time my eyes come down from watching the vagueness on the horizon, which takes Rio farther and farther astern and away. If I could cry I would, but out of nostalgic happiness at all the good times dear Rio provided me. It's like a young girl parting from her first crush, about whom she can only hope that they meet again, and soon.

JANUARY 7, 1912. (Very much at sea.)

Shifted sails to port side and headed NE by N, which, according to my study of the chart, is very good and should put us right on the

nose of Barbados. A splendid southeast trade wind, a bit lower in
latitude than we might have expected, is pushing us along toward
home. Fred's rheumatism is suffering from the intense activity of
discharging sawdust day and night. He works in the cold hold along
with the men, not only to lend a hand but also to show them that he's
not a dilettante follower but a real leader who shares the work with
his men. Also, I surmise that he knows they won't bellyache so
much when he's within hearing distance.

The young Norwegian sailor Fred robbed from one of the big
barks to replace Houghton doesn't understand too much English, so
Fred yells at him, apparently thinking that the louder one yells the
easier it is to be understood. The result, of course, is decreased
understanding because of the panic created by the noise. Mizzen sail
lowered to clean out after hold. All hands and the cook are at it, still
cursing. Ice residue rapidly melting, what with having lost the
sawdust covering. Fred says the men can have a holiday tomorrow
since the discharging is going so well. They'll just stand their normal
four hours on and four off, doing only their normal work, instead of
"Chinese watches," four on and stay on. Knowing my hubby, I can
see right through him. It's true that the sawdust is nearly cleaned
out, but the "holiday" will not be granted because of that; it will be
granted because the beautiful, fair wind is speeding us along so well
that we'd be losing time and money by not carrying every stitch of
sail we can hoist, so there's no profit in lowering one sail for taking
out the remaining sawdust. That will be done when the wind
slackens. Meanwhile, he appears as the benevolent master who has a
heart for his overworked slaves. But it's true that we are bowling
along like a yacht, and isn't it a wonderful feeling to cut with a great
clip through the sapphire sea, making long white waves off the bows
and astern, where the porpoises dive and blow in their race with us
and the flying fish dart and shine their many colors for only us to see
and marvel at in this paradise of pristine sea and benevolent sky of
deepest blue? The loveliness of it, buttressed by his success at the
uneventful and quick turnaround, make my boy so exuberantly
loving, despite his crippling rheumatism, that he holds me tight
every time he sees me and boyishly, as though he had never been

naughty, tells me he will always love me. Thank God for that, even though he's more in love with his good feelings of accomplishment, his ship and the sailing of it, than he is in love with anyone. I'm his audience, but I love to see him act. Never lose your reality, my girl, and enjoy him and his foibles. That may be wiser than being a moonstruck calf who might be a bit shaken when moods change such as might happen with a headwind. And make some chocolate ice cream. That will prolong the euphoria.

JANUARY 8, 1912.

Washed but no sun for hanging out clothes. Shed my lovely diamond ring for the first time, to wash, and felt the lack of it as I feel the lack of Rio. Wind continued fair, so no sails were lowered to take out sawdust. The old steward, carrying one of his priceless puddings aft, got tangled in some lines and spilled the pudding all over his dirty apron and the deck. He came aft, his fat belly wriggling as he laughed and told us, "Vee need a *bonde* aboard this hooker for me to get fore and aft. I shlipped on the shtays und de putting iss now kaput. Yah! yah! Dass iss very goot. De putting iss kaputting." Oh boy, oh joy.

JANUARY 10, 1912. (18 degrees south latitude. Calm all day.)

Washing finished and an indecent amount of ironing done. Last night Fred reminisced of Rio quite differently than I might have. Told of Captain Darrah once in Rio with Captain Rodin. Darrah was as unfaithful to his wife as was possible for one who hung about with Rodin. But then, are any sea-captains steady attendants at Sunday School? I never hear mine singing any hymns. Ah well, what I don't see won't hurt me, and when I do chance to think ugly thoughts, all I have to do is revert to Rio and my diamond ring and my Godgiven chance to get to know the world beyond the endless prairies, the great bores.

Why does the endless sea not bore as do the prairies, at least me?

JANUARY 12, 1912

Ship sighted to windward and that's a rarity on the prairies, daughter, unless you can call one of those ox-driven wagons a prairie schooner. After seeing real schooners! Bah. Let the gophers have all of the midwest, says I. But it does yield food, no doubt. Ah well, let those who want to raise crops for food enjoy it; I'll eat it while the great world is being seen by little old me. Am I selfish? I am.

One watch below for the first time since leaving Rio. How exhausted the men must be. And so am I after all that washing and ironing. And there's no shade on deck under the burning, red, penetrating sun. So to the cool of the cabin to rest and read that devil Kipling, who also saw the world with somewhat the same mental bifocals with which I see it. He wrote that the Colonel's Lady and Julie O'Grady were sisters under the skin, which I know but won't admit and then, he turned his eyes upward and wrote the beautiful *L'Envoi* in which, "Only the master shall praise us and only the master shall blame." That's me, my diary. From the depths of despondency to the heights of hilarity, all in one dog watch, I bounce like a ball. When, oh when, shall I ever grow up? Now knock off the analysis and get back to the grim reality of a balanced character, take the middle course for a moment. I shall take two or three more trips with my stud-boy, have my child brought safely into this world, bright and strong, sound of mind and body, and then heigh-ho, throwing my cap once again over the windmill, I shall get back to see the world, with Fred if he arranges the right charters to places like France and Spain and England and Turkey and landlocked Timbuctu, or without him. I can't let his exquisite nose act like a blind to my seeing things; it's his nose, not mine. Oh, but I do hope my baby has the same kind.

All this apparently brought on by Fred's spending half the

night telling me of that awful Goodspeed girl, she of the Boston culture, which must breed vermin. She must have been quite a bed gymnast. I told him to go back to her if that was what he wanted. Said I'd lived long enough in latin worlds to know that men were not monogamous, that every latin bride I knew expected to accommodate the horror of having her new husband soon tire of pure and good wedded love and run out to seek their old bedmates. He was taken aback at that like a ship suddenly encountering a squall. Did I really mean it? I said I couldn't find time away from the finer things of life to crawl through gutters. Fortunately, just at that time his fish line went taut and he sprang on deck, naked as birth, and became jubilant over a dolphin. That shows where his mind is, and his heart as well. Thank God for that fish!

I did not tell him I was two months' pregnant, because he would get some of that vile medicine in Barbados and I'd get sick and have no baby. I think he thinks he loves me, but he has the oddest way of showing it. A diamond is supposed to make amends for talk of Goodspeed and the other forty, but knowing what it's all about, merely an attempt to stimulate sexual activity, like reading lewd books, I twirl my diamond on my finger and let him rave on. Meanwhile I try to do what is right, and that means having my baby. Then I shall have everything.

And so, my girl, be "buxom, blithe and debonair," and "bring with thee jest and youthful jollity," especially, "quips and pranks and wanton wiles." Concentrate on the wiles, my daughter. It's a better way than a frontal resistance to a six-foot, two-inch sea captain with the power of a Russian Czar over his ship kingdom.

JANUARY 13, 1912

My suggestion that he feel free to associate with other women shook his Calvinistic facade of righteousness to his timbers. He has been moaning and groaning about how bad he was to me. I can stand the Victorian self-deception, for I know about Prince Edward going from brothel to high mass within the hour, but I shall let Fred writhe a bit. It's good for his soul. Basically he's just a healthy stallion and can't get enough, but when he plays Sunday School it revolts me and 'tis hard not to show it, although I must not let him know that I see too far through him. He must feel superior. And so the "wanton wiles."

At night under the moon I walked the after deck and brought my thoughts back to what I think makes Fred tick. In Port Clyde I noticed a bawdy, jolly, lusty, Elizabethan remnant now mixed with, but not thoroughly blended with, the Baptist code of conduct, which has been superimposed. The downeasters are not a colloid or a solvent into which the basics have lost their identity. One moment the lust comes out; the next moment it settles to the bottom of a crude mix and on top appears the righteous element. One moment the preacher is ridiculed as a "sky-pilot"; the next he is revered in the parlor on Sunday as the arbiter of who shall be saved.

One moment Fred and his sea-going peers from Maine are like the Squire in Fielding's *Tom Jones*, ready to roll in the hay with anything that can accommodate their lust; the next moment they boast of the stained window they gave the chapel. Their Sunday-go-to-meeting faces are shed as quickly as their blue serge suits and become goatish leers of pure corruption. The village is loaded with Lowells, Conants, and other old Puritan names, the descendants of the boys sent downeast from Plymouth and Boston and Salem to fish for the greater glory of those Lowells and Conants who stayed home and went to Harvard. The downeast cousins don't write much poetry, but their low brows outsmart the fish and their broad bottoms, low-slung to make good ballast for the dories, are more practical than the high brows of their sou'west relatives. If east met west, they could hardly communicate unless the talk was of herring. But amongst the villagers of Herring Gut are the Simmonses of black-eye "gypsy" stock, their ancestors said to have been rounded up by the agents of the Hanoverian kings and shipped as good riddance from around Bremen to Bremen, Maine, and the dour Scots-Irish who were brought over by the old English stock to man the quarries, the Lowells and Conants remained free of the enticements of emotional religion. They have no Congregational

Church as their Boston cousins do, the same church my Brewster and Moulton and Dorrance ancestors took west with them, but they have not succumbed to the extremes of the rest of Herring Gut, all Baptists if well-to-do and Advent if poor. The Lowells, Conants, Huppers, and Trussells keep what little religion they have strictly unemotional. If they are overheard humming a hymn, it is not "He walks with me and He talks with me," but something a bit less emotional, such as "Let the lower lights keep burning, send a gleam across the way. Some poor struggling seaman you may rescue, you may save." That hymn may have been written by one who wanted to entice seamen to be "saved" in a religious manner, but the descendants of the old English look upon it as strictly a lighthouse-keeping job to aid the sailor, whereas the emotional descendants of the Germans and the inheritors of Celtic underhanded rebelliousness against the English both cling to the feverish hope that supernatural allies will compensate for their lack of "git-up-and-git." Fred inherits the individuality and strong independence of his English ancestors but there has rubbed off on him, as on his mother and all the Huppers and Trussels, a bit of the wild and orgy-prone proclivities of the Germans and Celts, a sensuousness that is the other extreme of "holier-than-thou" religiosity. It is an addition to the old English Elizabethan jollity, and it results in what I'd call the third type of Maniac, aside from the coast and swamp categories, the sex Maniac.

So, my daughters, who read this in years to come: when at sea at night with a downeast skipper, never say yes when being wooed, especially when there's no other woman within a hundred miles, not counting seasick ones, like Betty. His lust will blind him to the faults or shortcomings, which he will later soberly see in you. For example, Fred expects me to spend all my time cleaning and picking up, when he should have known that I'd rather read. My room at college was a delightful pigsty. He expects me to couple with him at least once a night but, as much of a hedonist as I may feel at times, there are times when I'd rather hear an opera than participate in bedtime gymnastics. Never be too quick to give in to saying yes; wait until you've found out whether he expects you to be a ship-shape

cleaning woman daytimes and a bawd at night, and if he does, tell
him you're not signing on for more than one voyage. And don't be
overwhelmed by a lovely nose, although I know you will, being my
daughters.

JANUARY 13, 1912

Aren't my diamonds bright and how they do sparkle. Each time I
fondle the ring I think of the little, skull-capped Mendoza, the
Brazilian-Jewish jeweller, who picked out the finest of his lot for me
because he said I was *simpatica*. While Fred quibbled about the
price, Mendoza told me in Portuguese not to worry about the price,
that it would be low but he wanted to have some fun with Fred. He
had been impressed, days earlier when I visited his shop, by asking
him if he was any distant relative of the American Mendozas, which
he was. He was delighted that I knew the family history: Sephardic
Jews who were the backbone of Spanish banking, close advisors to
Charles the Fifth (Carlos Quinto), kicked out of Spain by Ferdinand
and Isabella's super-Catholic bureaucrats, welcomed, for a time, in
liberal Portugal, and then on to Amsterdam for asylum, whence to
Recife when the Dutch ruled northeast Brazil until they gave it up
when the sugar and slave trade became more profitable in the West
Indies and Georgia. The American Mendozas came from Recife to
settle in Newport, Rhode Island, managing the sugar imports and
the slave trade, then quite honorable, and helping finance supplies
for General Washington's poor troops at Valley Forge and Trenton.

JANUARY 14, 1912

Finally finished that awful washing and ironing. Glory be to the
Highest. Feel like sin, death, and destruction. Spinoza was one of
those Sephardics, like Mendoza. So was his philosopher peer,
Averoes. Brilliant, they were, and transmitting from Alexandria the
sacred Greek learning to southern Spain while northern Europe was
getting back out of barbarianism after the long eclipse of Roman

Too much?

culture ruined by the German and Asiatic tribes. Old Mendoza of
Rio had all that in his sorrowfully smiling eyes, and I'd go so far as to
say that you can see somewhat the same look on the face of young
Sadie Marcus of the Stonington Furniture Company in Rockland,
whose father, by the way, was a close friend of Captain John Hupper,
Fred's intelligent grandfather. Captain John helped Mr. Marcus get
going with his first store, which was at Port Clyde. Back in Squire
John's time, three factories were running, packing clams and fish,
and supplying the Grand Banks fisher fleet with ice and bait. Then
there were three shipyards and scores of vessels coming and going
with cordwood for the lime quarries, paving blocks for the
waterfronts of the world, and fish. Large squareriggers sailed out of
Thomaston for China and came home with gold and glory. John
Hupper's daguerrotype shows eyes that were *au par* to all of the
world and its activities, the same look one sees on old Mendoza's
face, and Sadie Marcus's. Isn't it wonderful to have your fingertips
on the pulse of the world's system?

The English founders of the Maine coast economy had that
feeling. On Bradford's Island, Gay's Island, Loud's, and scores of
others, the settlers' saltwater farms were stopping places for the
international trade in ideas as well as fish and ships. Aunt Ark-Ann
Marshall tells of her mother, back at the turn of the nineteenth
century, reading the bible in Greek and teaching the young girl
Latin. Her descendants, such as Orris Hupper's wife, follow that
tradition, but in a degenerate age surrounded by people who think
only of fish and filling their bellies and satisfying their sexual lusts,
people who are so far from ideas and Greek that they can hardly read
their D.C. Heath primers, and when they do, have to move their lips.
Orris's wife is an oddity. Can it be geography? The Herring Gut boy
of today is nearer the Penobscot Indian than his Jeffersonian greatgrandfather was. He knows where the fish will be before they do, and
he can stand hauling traps at four below zero, whereas scores of his
colonial ancestors holed up for the winter, some even returning to
England, as did the original Kennebec settlers. At any rate, Fred has
no taste for the things our mutual ancestors of the Plymouth,
Salem, and Massachusetts Bay colonial endeavors had. Did mine

benefit from going west and struggling through loneliness, thus relying on their inner selves, propagating intellectualism and clinging to the original respect for learning? Did his lose that lofty tradition in the rush for material gain? But our off-again, on-again contretemps is not all Fred's fault, my dear. I irritate him with my laziness, my talking too much of such things as opera, and I know I drive him wild when I protest at eating salt beef or salt mackerel for breakfast. Do I really believe the poor, darling boy could arrange fresh eggs at sea after we've been out months from land?

JANUARY 16, 1912. (33 West Longitude, 15-40 South Latitude.)

Offshore from where the American Mendozas had a sanctuary before the Dutch were forced from Brazil by the Spanish rulers of Portugal.

We tacked ship yesterday and stood off to the eastward with sail on the port side. Heading NNE, some two points more than is needed to get us around the eastern tip of South America with plenty of room to spare in case the westerly flowing currents are quite strong what with the southeast trades having been blowing rather strongly and steadily for this time of year. The mate "ain't much" but he knows his basic weather or, more likely "feels it." He says, "The current flows the way the wind blows," and I would never have believed it, but it is apparently true.

JANUARY 17, 1912

Going nowhere, very thoroughly. Same tack with strong headwinds. Steward made doughnuts. Like lead. Fred gobbled them. Wonderful shrimp salad for me. My ring is a consolation. For all my spiteful remarks about Herring Gut and the degeneration of sea-going descendants of my ancestors, I know that I would never have had such a ring had I stayed on my father's "intellectual farm." Maine waters send forth men who may not read without moving their lips, but they can hire or marry people who can. Is that so far from the old kings and nobles who fought and hunted but had to hire clerks to keep the records? Charlemagne could not read, but he was no ignoramus. Oh Dora! Now you're rationalizing. Please bring up your own children to be full people, both strong of mind and body.

JANUARY 18, 1912

Wrote some letters with my leaky fountain pen. Finished my tan linen gown. Out of antipathy to my natural slovenliness cleaned the bedroom but probably wouldn't have done so had I known how much there was to it.

JANUARY 20, 1912

Curried chicken for Sunday dinner! The only meal in the entire week that I might relish and enjoy but spoiled with all that abominable curry. Originally curry, like salt, was used to hide the taste of oncoming rottenness in meats, but users of it became addicted to it for its own taste. Fred insists I get used to it. Says I can't go to sea unless I learn to eat like a sailor. He honestly believes the stuff is a preservative against getting poisoned by old meat. And the way he commands, orders, that I like it. Just as he insists that I must become a bedtime acrobat. Just as he makes me drop my reading, all lies he says, to help him with his navigation and his accounts. I must drop everything and jump like a seaman when he speaks. If I don't jump and run, he gets that skipper's look in his eyes, which says, "Put her in irons and throw her in the lazarette." Really frightening until I remember that it's merely the second nature of one used to command. Then I stick out my tongue at him and he smiles. Cute? Maybe it's cute but it's also damned disturbing. My mama would call it adjusting. I call it conflict. He wants his ice tea strong enough to dissolve his throat. I want mine moderate. I make his strong and mine weak. He sips mine and says it's like his grandmother, old and weak. I say drink your own and don't meddle with mine. It's his turn to stick out his tongue. So far, no adjusting. Neither of us adjusts easily. So we shall see what happens. We shall see.

Now how, dear God, do I handle this latest mutiny? Out of spite at my wanting to sleep instead of put on a six-act Keith's vaudeville show in bed at three in the morning, he tells me that, although I'm two month's pregnant, he still does not want the child, yet. I say, "Then stop trying to have intercourse every change of watch." He says, "What's that got to do with having a baby." Says I, "Try having a baby without it." Says he, "None of your backslack." That's logic on board the *Hopkins*. So, to make my point I say, "Very well. I'll take some more of that foul stuff you had me take last year in Jacksonville, have another abortion, and peacefully die. Then you can marry a beefy, Boston Irish woman who is fit only for scrubbing and screwing." He then asks me what good books I have been reading lately. Last trick of the game to me, but it's rather an empty victory. Of course, when the baby arrives, it will be all his to fondle and teach crudities to. He'll probably have the baby slurping milk the way he does his pea soup. You'd think he was Chinese the way he plays a symphony in "I" Major whenever he eats. I hope the old steward is flattered; I'm not. I can't turn to anyone for understanding, let alone help, because all the creatures on board are completely and absolutely in his power. And that terribly vulgar deck of cards he acquired from Rodin in Rio! And lying openly on his desk, put there for me to see. Oh, did I ever see them! I waited for him to see me watching them. Then overboard they went, to show him. Then I found those ugly, pornographic letters written to no one by some perverted Englishman, someone called Frank Harris, and they followed the cards to the sharks. I'll be damned if I shall make ice cream for him tomorrow.

JANUARY 21, 1912. (Rounding Pernambuco. Course NNE.)

No other comment; said enough in yesterday's entry. Time for a bit of thought.

JANUARY 23, 1912. (34-26 West Longitude, 3-03 South Latitude)

Proper equator weather, sticky. Bathed in the lovely copper tub and felt better. Aired clothes on line and embroidered my linen pillowslip while enjoying the shade of the spanker from my deck chair on top of the house. Hubby on his knees below me painting the deck house. That's as it should be! But his contriteness is no better than his bullying and so I say steer the middle course, my dear. But he is not a Socrates, believing in moderation in all things. He couldn't be moderate even in moderation, if that makes any sense, which I don't believe it does. I'm as balmy as the weather. Oh God, what if I am, and he's right! That can never be.

To get my reason back, I packed things for sending to Port Clyde, things no longer necessary on board, including the Rio souvenirs, like the four little coffee spoons, beauties. Rather than accumulate treasures on board for my barbarian to ridicule, I shall discreetly but firmly start nesting away for shore leave during childbirth. Then I shall take over the best of the family houses, a small one, and fix it into a home for future refuge when the going gets rough. That way I can convalesce from him and be strong enough to put up with him at sea. The best of both worlds I shall have, damn his lovable nose!

JANUARY 24, 1912

Right smack on the equator and now, says Fred, it's all downhill sailing. "Hang on," he says.

Frosted steward's cake today, and when I looked up through the porthole saw Fred bent over with his rheumatism. Went on deck and saw that the idiot had on neither shoes nor stockings. I laid the law down, sounding like him, telling him to get dressed and stop being a poet. It sounded good to give him hell, and he grinned through his painful grimaces. My mother would have washed out

my mouth with soap and water. I seem to have the vocabulary down
rather pat, if I do say so.

JANUARY 25, 1912. (37-27 West Longitude, 0-09 North Latitude. Little headway.)

Ironed, of course, embroidered and mended, of course. Then came
the deluge. We had just gone to bed around midnight when there
came a white squall. I thought this craft would sink. Immediately I
remembered, in my panic, that I had questioned Fred about carrying
no ballast and his telling me that the southern seas this time of the
year were kind. Well, we nearly turned turtle. Fred dashed madly on
deck in nothing but what God gave him as a birthday suit. Dawson's
mate, Smith, was at the wheel. If Dawson had been on watch, it
might not have happened as he has an eye for squalls. But neither
Smith nor the mate saw the monster coming, as they should have.
The mate was all confused and shouted to let the topsails down. That
was like feeding a whisper to a gale. Fred acted magnificently. He let
go the spanker sheet to cut down the force of the wind upon us.
Then he let go the spanker topsail. It started to rain torrents. The
wind moderated. But this vessel rode along on her port side, the port
rail under water, too long for comfort. If Fred had not relieved her,
the ship would have surely tossed her sails into the water and,
wetting them, would have turned over.

Later Fred told the mate not to let a squall strike him like that
again so suddenly and so unpreparedly. "If you let that happen
again, I'll throw you overboard," he said. If Fred did throw him
overboard, no one would ever know what happened to him in that
dark pandemonium. Such is life at sea, and I suppose the mate ·vill
not be around next trip. Then Fred told me always to remember that
he never said any such thing. "Landsmen wouldn't understand," he
said.

Maybe Fred wasn't all wrong in talking of buying a farm. Maybe
I shall soon have all the going to sea I want. Maybe, but I doubt it.
I'll just watch out for white squalls and be a bit more insistent about

ballast. The sea may be nice, but it can also be treacherous, like a smooth-talking sailor, enticing.

JANUARY 29, 1912. (45 West Longitude, 3-17 North Latitude)

Ice all gone, cabbage all gone, one duck left. Hope to make Barbados a week today. Reading Newcomes, picked up in Rio from some English friends. Letters to Mother B., sister Nettie, Betty, and Mama. Fought with Fred, of course. Won, of course, but expect round two when we go to bed. Wish he would take up smoking, or even drinking in moderation. As he is, he's impossible. He needs a bit of weakening. Some say tobacco will do it. I shall get him some, but it'll probably be the wrong kind. Even if he likes it, the most he'll say in praise will be, "It ain't bad." That's downeast for "Wonderfully good."

FEBRUARY 1, 1912. (Within three hundred miles of Barbados)

Full moon tomorrow and that usually means two or three days of calm. Wish we might make Bridgetown and take our full moon calm there. Dawsie taught me more sealore. About squalls: "Come de rain afo' de win', take in sail and keep her in. Come de win' afo' de rain, man can put her out again."

Played checkers with Fred. His mind was on fish, so I defeated him twice. Then he got his vengeance by telling me, while washing, that I used too much soap. I said we weren't all that poor. He said that if we had anything, it wasn't from wasting things like soap. One trick for the New England mentality. I said I'd prefer to live in luxury. He said I should have been born rich instead of handsome. A second trick to Fred.

FEBRUARY 11, 1912. (Barbados.)

Some time since I have written here. It's a bother to write. Reached
Barbados Saturday morning after being thirty days out from Rio.
Took a pilot at the cost of one pound, five dollars. 'Tis a picturesque
little island but cannot equal the magnificence of Rio. Veddy, veddy
English, slow and quaint and rigidly mannered. Suppose you have
to search to extremes for any spontaneity; perhaps in the negro
quarter or the midnight parties of the drunken rich who can afford
to kick over the traces now and then. The elements we've run into so
far, shipchandlers and officials, all of the middle class, seem to be
half asleep and parroting primers of rightful convention. The
businessmen, eager to get commissions for arranging our business,
came out in bumboats. One, a Mr. Foster, outwitted his peers and
took us ashore. Went to American Consulate and got mail forwarded
from Rio. Photo of pretty sister Myra and cards from Captain J.W.
One card told Fred he was lucky to have me and ordered him to treat
me well. Father B. is chartered with coal from Baltimore to Fort-de-
France, Martinique at $2.00 a ton. Freights are up this year.

The consul is a Mr. Martin who was formerly at Martinique.
They're Michigan people and very kindly. We discovered that his
Martin ancestors were related to mine on my mother's side. "Isn't it
curious how all my people are kind and bright and good," I says to
Fred, "while yours are sour." Says Fred: "All you midwesterners
get on Uncle Sam's payroll, consuls and teachers, and get free land,
so why shouldn't you be carefree and happy. It's us easterners who
pay your way by working hard. We don't have time to be sweet and
kind, none, that is except me." I could have slammed him with the
large bunch of newspapers which came in our mail. Mr. Martin's
office is at his home, which has beautiful grounds, the garden walks
paved with coral. Fred says it's owned by our government, which he
supports so we should feel at home.

The shops close at two P.M., so had to rush to spend some

money, much to Fred's outward consternation but secret delight.
Drove out in a fringed victoria to the Fosters' for dinner and the
evening. Such succulent English roast mutton. Saw a polo match on
the old military training ground. Mr. F's home is one of the old
garrison buildings, made over. No troops stationed here now since
the Spanish have ceased, for two hundred years, in trying to take
Barbados back. Fred fidgeted all evening, because just as we left the
Hopkins he heard his fishline run out over the stern. He let out a yell
as though he was going to dive overboard and grapple with the fish.
At dinner he kept looking back at where the *Hopkins* is moored in the
stream, apparently anxious to get back before the fish liberated
itself. He didn't know whether he was eating delicious roast mutton
or salt mackerel. Fish are the only things that get any enthusiasm
out of that Herring Gut man. But, still, how he did eat!

On Sunday we hired a cab and went out to Cranes Hotel on the
white beach where the sand is as soft as Indian meal. A one-horse
cab it was, with a high seat for the coachman, and the gent was in
livery. Passed beautiful fertile plantations spotted here and there
with old Dutch windmills for irrigation. The winding road, lined
with flamboyans of red, cut through the gentle hills, which showed
small, white starflowers in their green. Had breakfast at ten and
lunch at two, after a swim in the breakers, and got back on board
early. Such typically English faces and dress on the people. Even the
blacks seem more English than the Londoners. Drove home along
the coast past Christchurch. There seems to be a Christchurch in
every English colony. I have read of one as far away as New Zealand.
The farther away the English get from England, the more English
they become.

Shopped on Monday and found such good things to eat. Our
main boom is being repaired but won't be ready until Tuesday, so we
get a chance for more sightseeing. Spent the day on shore. Visited
the consul's to clear the ship. Bought a pie-crust mahogany table for
my prospected home at Port Clyde. Sailed out into the calm and blue
and beautiful Caribbean on Tuesday, in the afternoon, and entered
Martinique harbor for a look-see for the *Margaret Thomas* and
Father B. Just like a vagabonding, yachting party sailing among the

islands. No sign of the *Margaret Thomas*. Sailed this fairy land and
sea of the Caribbean until Saturday night and then passed out into
the Atlantic by Sail Rock. Rough! Heavy seas slamming into us.
They have no islands to prevent them from increasing in force, out
here. Back in the lee of the Leeward Islands it was like a mill pond;
out here its like being in a waterwheel.

FEBRUARY 15, 1912. (All at sea!)

25-30 North Latitude; 71-40 West Longitude and bound for
Jacksonville to load railroad ties for Boston. Still six hundred miles
to go to Jacksonville.

Two very bad storms today. Old mainsail blew to shreds.
Spanker tied up, what with too much wind for it to handle. Lost two
jibs to Neptune. They blew away before we could get them in. Spent
part of the storms reading *Wee MacGregor*, a typically British book
from Barbados, but one long laugh. I shall send it to Myra, who will
enjoy it. Thank God for the laughs during the gale. But after the
wind went down up came the devil in Fred. Every time he gets out to
sea, after the concentration he must exert in port on ship's business
and after the delight he gets from shoving landsmen around to suit
his needs, he starts in on me. When I refuse to play the part of sea-
going concubine and assert my rights as an individual who refuses to
jump at his least whim, he dredges up the mud, which he knows I
despise, and does his damnedest to get my goat. Now its the baby,
which he knows I want so much. He talked of an abortion in
Jacksonville. That would make it two in one year. Not on your
tintype! What a horror that would be. He needs a child to soften his
hard heart and to give him something else to talk about beyond fish
and sexual intercourse. Isn't it strange that he shies away from the
intelligent guests I have on board — a poetess in Rio, Roxy Shaw,
the opera singer — and feels at home only with the harlots and
whores, such as Captain Rodin brought along with him. Fred says
no; he says whores and sailors go together naturally like codfish
with pork scraps; he likes to tell of scores of sailors who married

whores and found they made the best of wives. I can understand that
the girls might like a change from too much changing, but what I
don't like is his harping on it. I told him that I was beginning to
understand his great liberalism and his bohemianism. With a look of
wonder he asked me what that was. I told him I might change my
antipathy to divorce. "Who in hell is Auntie Pathy? Never heard of
her," he says. So long as he is prone to being confused like that I can
maintain the upper hand, but I mustn't laugh at him.

Last night I was having a good sleep and enjoying being cradled
by the gentle roll of the ship and being sung to by the sweep of the
wake just outside my bunk when enters my goatish hubby, hell bent
on what he calls, "A connection that will make you happy." I told
him I was quite content with things as they were and rolled over
away from him. That did it. He started talking about having Nellie
Atkinson on board in Boston. I know he wouldn't dare, but he had to
say something out of spite. So I returned the volley by telling him he
was a little boy who sulked and threatened and that I'd tell his
Daddy. His Daddy, I said, didn't want him to play with bad girls. I
knew, because his Daddy had written on one of the postcards that he
thought I was a brilliant catch for Fred. All that persiflage
unlimbered my stallion, and he went on deck to watch his fish lines,
but I could not sleep. I know that he once got Nellie in trouble and
paid the malpractitioner. He has tripped over his lines many times in
telling me of her when he was trying to get me feeling sexy. If he'd be
a bit tender and loving, less abrupt, he might get somewhere. The
brute doesn't have a snowball's chance in hell with me so long as he
barges in and thinks with his genitals instead of his head. Imagine
asking me to invite Betty for a trip! Imagine his look of awe when I
said, "*Ay! Que bueno. Porsupuesto. Yo me voy. Que goza del viaje con
ella.*" (Oh, what a beautiful idea. Of course. I'll go ashore and you
can enjoy the trip with her.) He didn't understand a word, but he got
the drift of the ridicule and shut up, puzzled. Then I told him that
for one so anxious to make babies, he was a bit off base to have them
killed. That stunned him. I pity the pipsqueak wives of downeast sea
captains who let themselves get worn out at sea and get sent ashore,
years later, as cast-offs. I shall not join that sorority and, in the end,

Fred will be proud and glad that I maintained my standards. But it can be hellish, meanwhile, and lots of fun as well. Don't give up the ship, Dora.

Sunday, FEBRUARY 18, 1912. (73 West Longitude, 28 North Latitude. Strong SW wind.)

Passed a government collier bound for the Panama Canal to increase the stockpile for bunkering the fleet with precious coal so that the navy Roosevelt built can show the world that America is the gem of the ocean, or is it Columbia. Fred is in sublime paradise, having caught two dolphins. I caught the steward preparing pork scraps and threw them overboard. Told him I'd buy him a beer in Jacksonville.

Friday, FEBRUARY 23, 1912. (Still at sea. Headwinds and heavy seas.)

Passed an American dreadnought and signalled to be reported. Calmer later but winds headed us offshore. In the evening a slight sou'west breeze allowed us to resume our course. Slow work ironing with only one iron. The other lept overboard out of the cauldron when the steward was trying to bring it aft from the galley stove. Embroidered a sofa pillow for Father B., whom I am falling in love with because he appreciates me, sight unseen. Must be a remarkable man, a real go-getter. At age twelve he went to sea as ship's boy on a mackerel-seining two-master, which chased the fish from Hatteras to Newfoundland. Come the following December when he was shanghaied back to school by his mother, in cahoots with the skipper, young Will came home one day to find five new, shiny ten-dollar bills stretched out on his bed. His mother told me, later, that it helped the family get over March Hill. It was his share in the summer's gross take of fish. From that to being captain of a two-master, the *Van Buren,* of the Hupper fleet, such a successful driver that he would make two trips to one made by Captains Sid or Joel Hupper, he was chosen by the daughter of the owner, Mother B., to carry on, as her husband; the drive and push of past generations was getting worn out and needed fresh blood. Fred is the overwhelming result. And disgustingly so!

FEBRUARY 24, 1912

Ninety miles to Jacksonville and in the middle of the Gulf Stream. Good morning sights, but rainy and typically Gulf Stream weather now. However, it's more pleasant than J-ville, to which I do not look forward one iota. I'll read until we set sail for Boston.

FEBRUARY 25, 1912

Tugboat and pilot alongside to take us in from the whistling buoy off which we anchored last night after breezing in through a thick fog and past an anchored steamer, something only Fred or his father would have the nerve to do. The ship's bell was struck at minute intervals all night while we lay at anchor, and its lovely toll made me sleep profoundly. This ship is mine!

The quarantine doctor has just been aboard. He says we're the cleanest ship he has seen in many moons. No fumigation or quarantine necessary. Hip, hip, hurrah, but there is Ali Baba and the Forty Thieves to confront, or customs.

FEBRUARY 28, 1912

Breezed through customs with my diamond ring on my finger, diamonds turned under. None of the forty thieves noticed it; too busy looking for dutiable booze. Stupid pilot took us to the wrong loading dock Sunday night, so we had to shift ship Monday bright and early. Now we're at Evan's dock, and ashore I did go. To church Sunday evening, where the place held together while I prayed for patience with my Fred and strength to rebel against any decree he might attempt concerning our child. My inherited Congregational blood steamed mightily as I resolved not to submit to irrational things like abortions, Baptist prudishness, and Fred's anti-intellectualism. Felt a beautiful cartharsis come over me with my resolve, and the beautiful music of the choir and lovely organ reinforced my determination to be myself. It was significant to me that the ladies in the congregation wore no hats; they are free of the silly conventions of all other sects, more like Unitarians.

Met Miss Foote and her beau coming out of the theater on my way back to the ship. Asked her on board for tea. With her came all the local gossip. Monday went ashore again and got loads of mail. Three letters from sister Nettie about her lost romance. She wants to get a loan to come east and take her master's degree at Columbia and then continue dedicating her life to teaching. Poor misguided dear. Three delayed Christmas packages. One card from Captain J.W., Captain Will, saying he "arrove" in Martinique. He probably gets arrove from arrive because a heaving line, once heaved, is "hove"; or is it because a driven oxen is drove? Anyhow I love the old English he acquired from his mother, she of the "Be ye from here or be ye from away." He was delayed on his trip to sunny Martinique by having been caught in the ice in upper Cheasapeake Bay for three long, gloomy, cold weeks. Poor dear, how he must have raged, cursed, and threatened.

FEBRUARY 15, 1912

Pump broke down again and holds flooded so could load no cargo. The lumber would get soaked, swell up, and bend. Started loading in the afternoon. Went on two auto rides in the same day, the first with the ship's agent down to the oyster country on the eastern shore, where Fred ate buckets, not just dozens, of enormous, luscious oysters, and I modestly confined myself to quarts. If it's true about what people say oysters do to sexual proclivities, God help us tonight.

Miss Foote stayed all night, apparently sent by God, for Fred stayed primly away from me to avoid any noise that might betray his animal lusts when approaching me in bed. As I felt the oysters — or do I imagine it? — I finally told him to chuck his modesty and come to bed. He was so surprised that he was absolutely kind and gentle. Of course, I took advantage of that to declare in soft, sweet words that anything approaching an abortion was beyond the wildest possibility; true to his character, either the commander or the little boy, he acquiesced. Not only another trick to Dora but also the whole blooming game!

Miss Foote likes the two Rio waistes I'd purchased for her, and gave me a check for them. Fred, with his usual perverted downeast sense of humor, let the check fall to the deck and, upon being asked by the dumbfounded Miss Foote, "What for?," said he wanted to see if it bounced. She brought us a primrose, and it's such a dear, sweet, lovely little flower. I told Fred he was being boorish, and I could see from his puzzled face that he thought I meant something to do with sex, he thinking of a boor in a pig's way, the poor illiterate dear. I must read to him more, like I shall do for my baby. Soon I shall have two babies on my hands.

FEBRUARY 29, 1912. (Leap Year)

Uptown, where purchased Norman Duncan's *Measure of a Man* and George Meredith's *Diana of the Crossways*. Went to a moving picture show and can't say I think much of them in comparison to opera or vaudeville. The Orpheum last Thursday had a wonderful quartet, and I enjoyed the acrobatic tumbling. Fred did, too, until I made a stupid remark about bedtime acrobatics. *Meti la pata.* [Editor's note: "I put my foot in my mouth."] Went as Miss Foote's guest to the Duval Theater, where saw *Every Woman*, and it was a good, perfectly splendid stage drama with a message so profound that it stayed with me and strengthened me better than a sermon might.

MARCH 8, 1912. (Over a week since my last entry.)

Now that I've temporarily gained the upper hand over Fred's lust by out-lusting him, just once, Jacksonville has become much less of a nightmare, and I have been so busy that I have given in to my detestation for writing instead of living, but, for my son and daughter and some imaginary posterity, the diary must be kept alive, so will note down briefly what has happened.

Spent nearly a day with Mrs. Hussey, she of the Friendship, Maine, Husseys, whose sea-going husband has become the chief of all shipping men in J-ville, the stevedore contractor, the tug owner, the manager of the pilots, everything but the boss of the sharks. Had a heavenly time listening to her darkie stories with a downeast accent. Laughed more at her, poor dear, than at her anecdotes. Got my new dress, and it is stunningly pretty and fits right in all the right places. Baked a cake for lunch when we go to Mandarin. Brightened up my cabin with more primroses to keep company with the lovely little one given us by Miss Foote. Called on Mrs. Lykes and saw her lovely furniture. Her family are shipowners, large fleets but nothing to compare with the Pendleton fleet of Isleboro, one of the biggest fleet of sailing ships in the world. Am I getting to be proud of Maine? Miss Foote and her beau of the brown eyes came to supper one evening. I must have developed an empathy for brown eyes when teaching my eighth grade at Utuado. Fred's are hazel. I love them, but they don't seem so outgoing and honest as brown. Mine own, being hopelessly blue, are without the pale for me. Drove with the Lykes under a beautiful blue sky, the color of my eyes, Fred said, to a fairy land of moss-covered oaks, gray and green, with here and there glorious red leaves shining out in their autumn glory, all in March. Seemed out of season, like Mother B's Rio strawberries. Under foot we trode on soft, mossy, swampy soil among the green lily fronds, so delicately colored. Florida is beautiful but so is Rio, which has more than just rustic beauty. How privileged I am to dwell in the best

spots on earth, the beautiful coast of Maine, exquisite Rio, exotic
Florida. Then there's always France and charming England, not to
speak of dirty but delightful Italy, all coming up on the horizon.
Unbeknownst to Fred, I've been working on Mr. Lykes for a charter
to carry some of his turpentine and pine masts to England with a call
on France to pick up wine for the return cargo. Scheming me also
thought, untold to others, of the rum factory of Don Jorge's family
that pays premium for barrels in which wine has been shipped.
They age the rum in wine hogsheads to give it an exquisite flavor, or
is it to hide the rank taste of rum? Anyhow, shall continue scheming
and hope it won't send Freddie boy up the spanker mast when he
finds out.

MARCH 16, 1912

So long since I've forced myself to keep notes for posterity. Thirty
times I've said, "The hell with posterity," but I shall now endeavor to
conscientiously relate the consecutive events. Drove to Mandarin
last Sunday. After shooing our many guests over the side on
Saturday evening, finished preparing for the picnic. Early Sunday
we beclothed ourselves in warm raiment of gentle blue and betook
ourselves to the tram, got off at the appointed spot, and, after a few
moment's waiting, who should appear but Mr. and Mrs. Irons with
their team of spanking sorrels, which pranced with us out on the
long but enchanting drive to Mandarin. How we Americans do name
our towns. Cairo, Illinois, pronounced "Karo," like the syrup;
Maine has Mexico, Peru, Norway, China, and God knows what else.
Now Florida comes along with Mandarin. It's a small, sleepy town of
deserted orange farms some twelve miles up the St. John's River from
J-ville. It was settled exclusively by exclusive British, a few of whom
still remain. Captain Miller has a small place there, which his wife
manages while he goes to sea to pay the deficit produced by the
oranges. She's a brave woman among the water moccasins and
copperheads and alligators, and very lovely. To get there we crossed

several rivers, some with bridges, many with fords shallow enough
and wide enough for the horses. They stopped to drink at each one. I
marvelled at the forests of live oaks and waded in the streams while
Mr. Irons rested the team. Fred was captivated into thoughts of
buying an orange farm, but, knowing him, I believe it is because he
adores eating oranges. We looked at various homes after Mrs.
Miller's aromatic coffee, with Fred buying each until I would slyly
bring up the question of deficits and declare that I was not one to be
neighborly with water moccasins while he went off to sea a-whoring.
Returned home without a farm and had tea at the Irons's in a
beautiful sunset over my sea, which sports dolphins instead of
moccasins. Wearily to bed, with Fred lecturing me on "being
decent." Nearly cried my eyes out early in the morning, because he
swore at me as he would at the commonest sailor. I can't stand such
treatment. Guess I'll have to try to be "decent," but come to think
of it, I really don't know how to.

Tuesday went to a matinee with Miss Foote. Saw a play called
Snobs. A very good company of troupers with Hy McIntyre as
leading man. "My uncle was so fat that when he fell down, he rocked
himself to sleep before he could get up." Good, breezy play.
Wednesday towed down the river and went to sea, but the good
breeze died out before we could make seaway and get off soundings,
so we anchored to wait for more wind. Hereabouts the counter-
currents of the Gulf Stream can set you southerly, and that was the
way we did not want to go. Thursday the tug *Three Friends* came to
see if we wanted a tow outside, but Fred was feeling poor. To join
him in his mood I washed clothes, and, fortunately, the breeze
sprang up to relieve me and off to sea we did sail with spirits high.
Damn the wash!

Sunday, MARCH 17, 1912. (Between Capes Romaine and Hatteras on the inner edge of the Gulf Stream.)

All hands and the cook anxious to get to Beantown. Began baby's
outfit as a token to the Gods, who strengthened me in J-ville against

the abortion, which, God be praised, Fred did not mention. The joy has made me balmy, and so the petticoat I made yesterday for baby is almost big enough for me to wear. Passed two steamers bound south and, wouldn't you know it, headwinds. Washed glasses. The old steward is so blind he can't see the dirt he left on them. He probably is not so blind as careless.

MARCH 18, 1912. (Passed Cape Hatteras yesterday P.M. Very calm.)

Read *Prodigal Judge* yesterday. Very interesting plot with three threads, all well handled. Somehow one feels as though the author might have used his talents more sanely and wholesomely in a story of more substance. It's as though Tennyson wrote doggerel. But I do hear — from whom? — that Kipling did not get the Poet Laureateship because he wrote such obscene but witty pieces as *The Bastard King of England.* I do hope he did, because it's a wonderfully witty thing. Why does so much humor come from the great poets under nom-de-plumes? Now take that bawdy song about the Kennebec whore, which I overheard on board the paddle-wheeled steamer running from Portland to Boothbay. That's a gem of a poem but completely orphaned. Was it Longfellow, Whittier, Bryant, or Lowell? They'd never acknowledge it, although it has real genius. Perhaps someday we Americans will become more open about some of the basic facts of life, which are certainly here to stay.

MARCH 22, 1912

Calm and bright just about fifty miles south of Montauk Point. Fred fishing while the sails slat, I hanging out wash on the line, finishing my embroidery in the deck chair, wrapping up Father B's table mat and generally being thoughtful about Mary Johnson's *Lewis Rand* and the way she handled the character development in the story, the rise and fall and final salvation of Lewis Rand. Such sparkling conversation, lucidly written. The most touching thing is Jacqueline's heroic devotion to her husband. Would that there were

more such women today. Baked marble cakes Thursday, and Fred
saw to it that not one crumb was left six hours later to tell the story.
That's devotion!

MARCH 26, 1912. (Boston, would you believe it! I can't, quite.)

Such luck! Last week was simply awful, enough to cure the worst
case of sea-fever, but not mine. Gales and the highest seas I ever saw.
The *Hopkins,* light and tiddly, would climb up a solid mountain of
water, up and up until her jibboom was invading the heavens, right
straight above us; then down, down, plunging downhill into the
depths on the other side of continuous mountains, until she
shuddered and shook and submarined half her length. And me
trying to wash clothes! It might have been terrifying if we all had not
known that she was a Thomaston-built schooner, put together by
the best men in the trade, such as Oliver Ames, the Washburns, the
Lermonds, with old techniques absorbed from years of building
them for the typhoons, gales, and hurricanes that confronted, for
hundreds of years, the sea-going men of the "Town That Went to
Sea."

We made light vessel #90 Sunday in the rain and fog, and
anchored off Gay Head. Monday we beat up Vineyard Sound, tacking
frequently. Then we anchored, tired out, and went ashore in the
launch to buy some coal for the galley stove. Tuesday a towboat
ordered by Crowell and Thurlow, as soon as they had learned our
whereabouts, came alongside us, and now we are towing to Boston,
hoping to get there early in the morning so as to dock before ebb tide.
A fine, fair wind and some sails still set. At Vineyard Haven, there
was no bituminous coal; it was all "nailed" on account of the
threatening coal strike. Finally, we purchased some anthracite, and,
as the poor engineer says, "Guess I won't have time to read any of
your books, m'am, with that coal needing stoking every two

minutes." How good the fresh meat and eggs and apples taste after the southern fare of grits and hominy and paw-paws. Out from J-ville two weeks tomorrow, and that makes the fresh food taste even better. The towboat bill of two hundred dollars is driving my boy daffy. Crew is unchaining the deckload of lumber. Knowing this treacherous area, I think it's a bit early. We might get a nor'wester yet and be blown to hell out past Nova Scotia. This vessel has made $11,400 freight money on this round trip to Rio and back. Not so bad, so please God no nor'wester to spoil Fred's great success with costly delays just when he is feeling good. I hear we may be chartered for Aguirre with molasses for some port as yet unknown. Do the French eat molasses? I must buck up my spirits for Aguirre, with its droves of Fred's old friends, including the shady ladies. Always the spectre walks before me, but now I'm learning how to handle it. If he didn't lie so, first when bragging about his conquests to stimulate me into sexual activity, when he should realize that such braggadacio is cold water to me, and secondly, when telling me my acrobatics are lacking in comparison to others. It's so easy for a man to lie to his wife about such things, and it's so easy for a wife to be a fool and listen. I shall find ways of treating it as mere boyishness or a lack of Baptist righteousness or something else. It's like the Kennebec logger who must jump across the river from ice cake to ice cake, always alert. Stay alert, my dear, and stay reasonably happy in the precious empire you have carved out for yourself.

Have made one little slip and two petticoats for my infant's wardrobe. I shall buy some slips and flannels in Boston, ready made. Shall also get some pregnant gowns and wraps for myself. The puffier the better, to show Fred what he's up against; then, when I want to relieve him, I can shed them and won't he be surprised to find little me behind the facade. You're a devil, Dora, but isn't it fun.

Mailed some letters in the Vineyard yesterday but must write more. If you don't write them, you don't receive them, and aren't letters a joy when entering port. Then, of course, it's a great yen my friends and relatives have for news of their wayward Dora.

APRIL 8, 1912

Went to Tremont Temple Baptist Church last Sunday, which was
Palm Sunday. There was a good choir, with many obviously Celtic
tenors, probably Scots-Irish protestants from northern Ireland. God
knows Boston needs such a counter balance to the hordes of
Catholic Irish, who seem to breed like rabbits and are entering all
walks of Boston life. The music was splendid, but the basic
fundamentalism of the Baptists peeked through the good music
enough to disturb me, so I took a streetcar out to Harvard and
Radcliffe to look up some old friends. Got myself carte blanche for
the Harvard libraries. Saw two ex-classmates from the University of
Minnesota, who are doing graduate work at Radcliffe, using
Harvard facilities. Saw in the library some documents regarding my
Brewster, Dorrance, and Putnam ancestors. The Luther Martin
tribe is so profusely recorded that I merely took notes of where to
research them in the future. Found I had seven ancestors fighting in
the Revolutionary War, none of them eminent, except General
Putnam, he of Bunker or Breed's Hill. Discovered that Fred's
Hupper tribe originally settled in Marblehead, as did many other
families from the Channel Islands. A mixed breed they were, which
accounts for their French noses. Their tallness probably comes from
Viking invasions of those handy islands, as does their wanderlust
and adeptness at sea-going; to say nothing of their smuggling
proclivities. Captain J.W. is moderately notorious for smuggling
guns at every port he visits. Seems to me it must be dangerous,
mixing with that sort of people.

Mother B. arrived from Port Clyde yesterday on the Bangor-
Boston steamer. Not so jolly as I remember her from our last visit,
she was complaining about everything: the steamer wasn't sailed
properly, the food was not to her liking, Fred's present of good
Brazilian beer was not the porter she wanted. And so on. Believe I'll
steer clear of that lady and give her the widest berth I can until she

moderates. Imagine telling me that my information about the name
Monhegan was all wrong! 'Tis not an Indian name, she said, but
merely an expression evoked of an Indian who landed on the island
and found the Breton fisherman gone. Says Mother B.: "The Indian
looked about and said, 'Man he gone.' That's how the island got its
name." Now I say!

Captain and Mrs. Darrah had us on board their vessel for
Saturday evening supper of baked beans and brown bread. They had
purchased daffodils for me to take back aboard the *Hopkins*. Alice
Balano's husband, Herbert Davidson, came aboard to visit. A fond
memory of our wedding, which he so efficiently arranged while Fred
hung back and combed the waterfront for a cook. Or was Fred
having last-minute regrets and trying to find some accident that
would prevent his getting shackled? Mr. Henderson of the literary
craft on board and talking of having his reporter daughter, just out
of Radcliffe, make a trip with us "for the experience." Oh, the poor,
dear girl. Experience is what she will get! She's a most interesting
young girl, and a reporter on the *Herald* staff. She is incessantly
curious and questioning and follows Fred about like a dog,
fortunately not panting but seeking erudition. He's about as good a
source for reliable information as his mother was when explaining
Monhegan's name. Miss. H. asked the names of the seven masts of
the *Thomas Lawson*. Says Fred, "Oh, just call them by the days of
the week." It took Dawsie to tell her the truth: "Deys de fore, main,
mizzen, jigger, driver, pusher, and spanker, missie."

We go not to Aguirre, praise the Lord, but are chartered for
Humacao, Menabo, and Arroyo and expect to sail around the 15th.
Fred doesn't like to go to Humacao. Not only because it is too far
east and may require beating to windward if we first load in a port to
the westward, but also because it brings back an episode he would
like to forget. It seems that his first command, the four-master
Mabel Jordan, was given him in his early twenties but with the
stipulation from his father that he keep the old mate on board to
serve not only as mate but as councillor on major decisions. The
mate counselled Fred to sail close to the Puerto Rican coast when
swinging around the eastern end off Fajardo instead of doing what

Captain Arthur Elliott of Thomaston had advised Fred, that is, to steer well clear of the land because currents set shoreward, and, in a calm, the ship might be set ashore on that rocky coastline. She was, and was lost. I got this story from Dan Sullivan, the lawyer who handled the case for Fred against the insurance companies. Fred took several years to recover. That's when he sailed mate with Captain Fales, refusing to go back as mate with his father, who might remind Fred, at impossible moments, of the tragedy. I shall never mention it to Fred.

Saw Gertrude Elliot yesterday afternoon in a play by Pinero, *The Indiscretion of Mr. Panmure,* rather a delight and with good dialogue, but slight. There's a terrible truth underlying it all: that whether the girl is guiltless or not, in any indiscretion, the man goes scot free. The girl always gets the blame. In simple terms, there's no such thing as seduction or rape. It raised the hackles of my midwest upbringing. Out where men treat women as something special, probably because there are so few of them, one would never hear such. Of course, in the mining camps, farther west, its different, but for homesteaders a woman is too rare and precious to maltreat.

Letters from Minnesota, and all seems to be well there. They have been reading the books I sent them about the sea and are beginning to understand *Two Years Before The Mast* as something real, now that daughter Dora is well into her second year before the mast. Father has been appointed justice of the peace, or do they elect them? Mother is hell bent to get her W.C.T.U. chapter behind some politician named Volstead, who must have had an awful drunk somewhere in his family tree; he's so avid to do away with drink. Instead, he ought to travel a bit and see that the best solution is moderation, which can be taught in the family. I shall let my children have a bit of wine now and then and, as the wise Catholics and Episcopalians say, "Drink to the greater glory of God."

Grand Opera in Italian last Friday evening, *Girl from the Golden West.* Destim is a soprano of great range, and Amato was wonderful with his deep baritone. Zenatello is a rare tenor. I loved every breath of it, and am resolved to buy a gramaphone so my favorite operas can be played at sea. That'll keep Fred on deck!

APRIL 10, 1912

It is beginning to seem that I never write in here unless I feel down. I insisted on going to see *Billie Burke*, got tickets for the matinee. Fred would not go and wanted me to take his mother. She was impossible. The coachman didn't know how to drive the horse to the theater; the theater was too hot; the music was too loud; the costumes were too scanty; the conversation was foolish; the thanks I got was her finding fault with me for wasting money on silly frivolities. I asked her, sugar-sweet, if she would have been better off staying back in Herring Gut and going to a "time" at the Knights of Pythias Hall. She said that was for "them others," not for her. "My home suits me fine," she said. She was so disgustingly harrying and so sour that I took her for sweets to a little parlor on Washington Street, where I buttressed myself with a glass of wine. She said that no one going to sea should pay such a price for wine, when they could just siphon off a noggin from the casks on board the ship; those, I suppose she meant, hidden away from some past trip. Then she asked for a glass of wine, too, and had a second. I took fiendish advantage of her at that, telling her the Latins had a most intelligent attitude towards wines, food, and other goodies. "They have a saying," I said, "*de lo bueno, poco*. It means, 'Of good things, take only a little. It can also mean that one should be moderate in all things, such as criticizing plays.'" she sputtered something about people being too smart for their own britches, and we went back to the ship, she grinning and I reliving the delightful play. Billie Burke is a dainty, delightful girl, vivacious, dear and sweetly blonde. The four-act comedy about Collette's aunt wanting her to marry the mayor's son, who is a semi-idiot, presents a relief of vivacity against the primness of the old ladies, who are shocked by Collette, who runs away and takes refuge with a Parisian artist, old enough to be her grandfather. But he's a great, good, and noble man, saving her. They're truly in love and marry before the aunts and crazy Pingo can hurt her. All good actors

and clever lines. The therapy was also good for me, getting me away
from those distractions of Fred and his mother, which don't lend
moderation to baby's development. I need calmness for my child to
be born in good shape, and there's no chance for that with Mother B.
about. God knows she's a good woman, and I don't want to get to
hate her, so the best thing to do is to avoid her. You don't do that by
taking her into account, not even when she's sitting beside you at
the theatre, jawing away. I made the mistake of telling her at
intermission about the research I'd done on her ancestors.

"What did you want to do that for?"

"It's interesting."

"Where they come from don't bother me none," she said.

It reminds me of the story they tell about her back in Port
Clyde, the one of her and the parson who came to call on Sunday and
sat with her in the parlor, open that day only. Says the parson,
distraught with the heavy silence; "Nice sheep you got out in the
yard, Mrs. Balano." Says she, "They look all right on this side."
Careful Caroline, she's called, hanging on to not every penny but
every word, as well. If that's how to accumulate money, I'll settle for
a garret in Paris with hard cheese and watered absinthe.

And worst of it is that when she's around Fred, he is mama's
dutiful little boy, "yessing" her to kingdom come and siding with
her against my "jest and youthful jollity." Nothing I do or say is
acceptable to their conspiracy to beat me down to their penny-
pinching show. Yet, when either of them wants something, I'm the
one to go running. And whatever I do is either wrong or odd or
queer. All the thanks I got for making tea was that it was too weak for
him and too strong for her. To hell with both of them; I'll see every
show in town while they stare at each other and count their shares in
vessels. That way someone will get some use out of the filthy lucre
they've saved by giving messengerboys rotten apples and sailors
wormy biscuits.

APRIL 14, 1912

Yesterday at matinee to see Donald Brian in *The Siren*. Written by
the author of the *Dollar Princess*, it has a company of one hundred.

The scene is laid in fabulous Venice. It has a very slight but intriguing plot, which holds together some poems of love written to the Queen, whose King finally discovers them and recognizes the author, who is banished but later forgiven and allowed to wed Lolette, whom he was after all along but used the strategem to startle the lethargic King, or Duke, into giving Lolotte her freedom by showing that the Queen was more suitable to him than Lolotte. The show had a very striking waltz, the "Valse Caprice," sung ecstatically by Brian and Miss Julia Sanderson; also a two-step sung by two minor actors. "Oh do step the two step," so light and catchy. Gay songs with the chorus dancing and, in the opening scene, "I always come back to you." A fat couple furnish the comic element, he a veterinary surgeon, and poor Lolotte calls him a horse doctor, while he sings, pathetically off-key, "I want to sing in opera."

After the show, I ran into Miss Henderson and we sipped a glass of inspiring madeira while I acceded to her desire to learn about the sea by teaching her the rules of the road in Dawsie's verse:

When on de starboard red is seen, well on de bow before de beam,
Port, beware, reduce de speed.
De red light had de right of way, de law command; you mus' obey.
and:
Green to green, red to red
Perfect safety, go ahead.

Husband says no new boots for me. You just watch me get them. Will he ever go ashore with me? Is he ashamed to be his usual generous self when his mother is watching? I am beginning to believe that his natural generosity is contraverted by memories of the training she gave him. Captain J.W., being a generous person, should never have left Fred at home as a boy to assimilate her penuriousness. Captain Will has spent wisely and well, over her opposition at every step, otherwise the family would not own the waterworks supplying the village or the tenements built of old dunnage or the many income-producing investments in assets other than the old hulks, onto which the Huppers hang when everyone with half an eye can see that sailing vessels are doomed and steamers are the future. Captain Will has shares in many a steamer, although he loves sail, but the Huppers can't see beyond the bowsprit of a three-master. She nearly climbed the spanker when she heard that her husband had put a thousand dollars into Sosthene Behn's new-fangled Puerto Rican telephone company. It's now paying well and doubling value every few months, but she just knows it is money poured overboard. Oh, well, I shall stay in my cabin with my diary and read the new *Saturday Evening Post* for mirth and the *Outlook* for catching up on the world. Ought to write some letters, but don't want my mother-in-law's jaundice to seep into them.

APRIL 18, 1912.

Towed over to the molasses dock to load shooks [Editor's note: shooks are unassembled barrels or hogsheads].

Four first-class battleships at Boston Navy Yard, the biggest drydock on the coast. Also a cruiser and some cutters. With the manner in which Kaiser Bill is acting now that he has fired Bismark, we shall need a fleet. The foolish boy was controlled by his great statesman until recently, but now he is madly interfering in Morocco after his shameful backing down in the South Seas when the English backed the Americans against the German fleet. If there's trouble and war, I doubt Fred will be prepared; all he thinks of when I say we must prepare is that the authorities in Washington may not let the old steward go to sea with us. That's international awareness!

Such a terrible maritime disaster last Monday evening. The *Titanic* of the White Star Line, largest steamer afloat, struck an iceberg off Newfoundland, on her maiden trip to New York. Only about one-third of the crew and passengers saved. The rest drowned with the ship. Everyone is much a-stir over the news. Fred says that's what they get for building them with "all top and no bottom."

Glorious day! Mother B. sailed home! Father B. "arrove" in Baltimore Tuesday, and we tried to get her to go on and visit him. "I've served my time," she said, "and my home suits me fine." She made some remark about the stewardess he has on board, and I suppose the poor old gent just has to find consolation somewhere. She did not thank Fred for the lovely amber beads we gave her, nor did she kiss him goodbye when she was hoisted up the gangway on the Bangor boat. It's eerily unnatural and I, who am supposed to live with her during my pre-hospital pregnancy and until I can furnish the lovely little house I've chosen for my own, shall have to be wary that her spleen does not enter my unborn baby's milk.

Twas the eighteenth of April in seventy-five
And hardly a man is now alive who remembers that famous day and year,
But Mother B. is gone, she took a dive
And Fred has become a perfect dear.

Wouldn't you know it; Dora's a po-it! Wrote some letters in that mood and all my friends won't know the woes I've suffered, praise the Lord.

We may get away Saturday to sea. If not we may go to New York and spend the day with Father B., which would be great. I wrote him yesterday that I'd love to see him. Fred took a goodly share in Crowell and Thurlow's new steamer. That's progress. His mother would have told him to keep it in the bank. I told him to take it out. The poor darling is caught between Hupper hoarding and Moulton munificance. But Captain J.W. will be glad to hear that Fred has slipped moorings from his mother's backwardness. Captain Kent is to be master of the new steamer and has asked Fred to come with him so as to prepare for being master of the next steamer. She's to be completed early next year.

Had my classmates who are now studying at Radcliffe, Frances and Marion, on board for tea and those sweet but very practical girls asked me to stop wasting my time on my diary and write a book about my travels. From the poetry I write, I guess I'd better not. I'm too prone to write what the publishers would never print.

Had my Rio photos framed and shall take one on board for hanging in the cabin; the rest are bound for my hideaway in Herring Gut to devour while I'm home and Fred is abroad.

Tuesday evening heard the N.Y. Metropolitan Opera Company do *Koenigskinder*, first time ever played here. Geraldine Farrar made the Goose Girl strong and sweet at the same time. Slender, blonde, and beautiful, she hails from Melrose. Carl Jorn is wonderful as the King's son but Goritz, the itinerant fiddler, showed more power in his voice and more promise than any of the others. The large and splendidly conducted orchestra was strong both in crescendo and retard. There were many motifs and several catchy peasant songs in this fairy opera so typically German with schmalz. How can such a sentimental people fight so much? Humperdinck took three years to write the opera. To say I enjoyed every minute of the long opera would be putting it mildly. Aside from the beautiful music and lines and costumes, I enjoyed the escape from Mother B. and the rest of the world's sordidness, as a little Dora, age nine. Some might say that's unrealistic, but I find it very healthy to participate in God-given reliefs from baseness if for no other reason than to be fortified in facing them.

So my dear children and grandchildren, at the risk of boring you blue, I give you the story of the opera, which reinforced me so that I might make myself strong enough to give you not only birth but also brightness:

The Goose Girl, of royal parentage, has been reared by the witch in poverty. The King's son wooes her, but can't beat the spell cast by the witch. She cannot break away from the witch, although she loves the Prince. The fiddler and his merry companions come to inquire of her who should be their ruler. He it is who urges the Goose Girl to cast off the spell and go to the Prince with his crown on her head, the fiddler having preempted the crown for her to wear. In a trance she answers that the next person who enters the city's gates shall be the next ruler.

The second act is very different from the first. It is set in a village where many people are dancing and Jorn is at his best. Among the throng is the stout, jolly inn-keeper and many royal councillors and courtiers. The Prince, unrecognized, is bewailing his sad state but decides to establish his kingly prerogatives and assume the crown. The fiddler brings to him the beautiful Goose Girl. A little peasant child is the only one who, enchanted, sees in the Prince and the Goose Girl the real, good, and lawful rulers. The King's son and the Goose Girl depart together.

The third act is sad. The witch has died. The fiddler lives solemnly in a hut. The King and Queen, wandering hungrily about the country, despised, trade their crowns for a loaf of bread and forthwith die while lovely Geraldine sings, "Ich liebe dich." Perfect schmalz and I drank in every sentimental note so thirsty was I for something better than salt beef, crudities, and Mother B.'s ungraciousness. Went out and got tickets for Lohengrin, as I intend to stay on this drunk until we sail.

APRIL 25, 1912. (Bound for Puerto Rico. Fair and strong S.W. winds.)

Miss Henderson seasick and I sewing on Fred's blue shirt while sitting in my deckchair atop the house, where it is very pleasant watching the ships pass us on their way to Boston. Only one new man in the crew, the mate; Fred claims this is because the *Hopkins* is known as a lucky vessel and also one of the few on which the skipper provides fresh fruits and vegetables. The rest, methinks, must be pretty bad. The steamers, with their refrigerated compartments for food, must be better. Today passed a beautiful bark, and my heart is torn between the beauty of sail and the bounty of steam. How I do love sail, the white of the canvas against the yellow pine masts, all lighted by the sun over a sparkling blue sea, a glorious symphony of color.

APRIL 28, 1912. (67 West Longtitude; 36 North Latitude. Full moon, calm. Horrors.)

In the midst of our jubilation about having a quick, good run comes this full moon calm. Here we are south of Bermuda in no time at all, with only ten degrees to make for southing, and no N.E. trades to keep us from drifting eastward. After a very calm twenty-four hours, however, a slight breeze sprang up from the southwest, and so we celebrated with canned asparagus, most savory. Reminded me of our visit with Father B., who said, contrasting modern conveniences on shipboard with those of a generation ago, "Nowadays I don't ship a cook so much as a can-opener." He once served as cook on a fishing schooner and spent twenty hours a day keeping the fishermen stuffed. To this day he is a remarkably fine cook and epicure who loves good food, well prepared. I love him. He has nothing tawdry or shoddy about him but can be wholesomely bawdy. At fifty-eight he has not one cavity in his beautiful teeth, stands his own watch at sea even though he can afford several mates. He loves to handle the ship himself or else he'd be ashore managing the fleet. He'd better, soon, or the clerks, under Mother B.'s parsimonious hands, will so stint on repairs and maintenance that there'll be no fleet.

Miss Henderson is sunning herself on deck between hard swallows and trips, now less frequent, to the rail. Dawsie explained why she should go to leeward for that. He calls it "loooard," and she told me she thought he said "lewd." It didn't make sense to her, she said, "but neither does anything else, right now." The poor *Boston Herald* is not getting much out of her. She sighted a cockroach in her stateroom, filled it with roach powder, climbed into my hammock on deck, and the swaying of it made her sicker than ever. Fred said the cockroaches love the powder, and, sure enough, there were several more this morning when the steward cleaned her room. The poor child. Fred told her not to kill Herman, the ship's mascot cockroach, and she fairly shrivelled.

Made a little slip for Baby's wardrobe with the little strength remaining in me from my trying to contain my cruel laughter at Miss Henderson's tribulations. Haven't much strength anyway, what with the baby taking it all, but what care I so long as it is a good, healthy, and bright little baby, with a nose like its papa's.

For the tenth time, Dora, write some letters.

MAY 2, 1912.

Four hundred miles to go to Humacao, according to my sights; four hundred and one according to my conservative, downeast spouse. Does my sextant cheat to give me the impression we're doing better than we are? Fred doesn't like Humacao, wants to go to Aguirre. Humacao is too shoal, he says, and too far east. He doesn't want to have to spent several days beating to windward, nor do I.

Have washed and ironed for three days straight, and tomorrow is Friday with still some garments unironed. Why can't people go naked. Am enjoying respites from ironing by doing my baby's layette, little checkered dimity dress today, a princess type, which I hope I shall turn into a prince type, but it's easier to trim off lace than to tack it on if he is a girl. Put down new linoleum on dining saloon deck, a great improvement. Also salved Miss Henderson's sunburn; she's beet red and blistered, and I don't see how she can be enjoying her trip, but she says she is. I hope so, because she's taking such an interest in baby B. and is such a dear person.

Hot. I have no more appetite, for once, than a rock and twice as much gas as Vesuvius. Mother never told me about this part of pregnancy. Fred flirting with Miss Henderson, the old goat, but she's too sunburned to reciprocate, thank God. I don't want to laugh at him but I can't help it. He's so obvious and so left-footed. To flatter her, he said she looked like a boiled lobster!

MAY 3, 1912.

61-52 Longitude says Fred, and I say 62-01, with just 300 miles more southing to make and 180 miles to beat to the westward if the trade winds, upon which we based our hopes, do not materialize. We had assumed they would head us off about here, and so we slanted east to take advantage of the good westerly breezes to put us into the N.E. trades. If they don't come, we'll make a slow passage, beating west, damn it. Time to whistle for wind, since we have no more old shoes to sacrifice. Fred is charming now that baby is a fait accompli; says if it's a girl we shall name it for me; if it's a boy, for him or his father, James Wilfred. I think Fred Moulton Balano would be a lovely name. I told him that for economy's sake, I'd like twins and save going through this ordeal again. One boy and one girl would make everyone satisfied. Speaking of being satisfied, I forgot to tell you, diary, about the little Shaw boy in Rio and the *bonde* he takes to school. It seems one mealtime he told his mother he was full, in Portuguese. In that tongue it's more polite to say, "My appetite is satisfied." The next day he was late from school and gave as an excuse that *o bonde estava satisfeito*, the tram was satisfied, too full.

Sunday, MAY 5, 1912.

Thirteen days out from Boston and anxious to get in. Wonder if Captain Kreiger has arrived. He ought to have, because he sailed two days before we did. His lovely wife, Jennie Flood Kreiger, is to have a vessel named for her and Captain Billy will sail her. That's one launching I won't miss. She is such a determined downeaster, the best, that I can imagine her chasing the vessel down the ways with the champagne bottle and swimming out to christen her, saying a ship should only be christened when afloat.

The old steward just came aft with a tiny black derby on his spreading white locks, looking like a late edition of Puck, and said I was to tell "that domned Fred" that the baby would need a nurse and that he, the old steward, knew all about nursing from having been Fred's. "I think I make a better yob dis next time."

Miss Henderson taught me a new fudge recipe, using Karo syrup instead of water. It's chewier than the other and not so sickenly sweet. Made some for a trial run, and Fred said, "It warn't bad, just a mite sour." If he doesn't end up with sugar diabetes, I'll never know why. So far, baby's outfit has cost the whole sum of ten dollars, nightgowns, flannels, diaper cloth. It will need another ten dollars and five more for mine.

Took some medicine yesterday and feel better today. Finished reading *Recording Angel* in the *Post* by Mrs. C.L. Harris, who does a good job, with style, on characters of ordinary interest. They come alive, even the humdrum ones, like I wish my diary would come alive with such mundane entries as washing, ironing, and asparagus. I'm sure my children will never get beyond page one in this diary of mine, but I really don't care, because it has served me well to record my thoughts, my spites, and some things to look back upon, such as *o meu Rio, amor meu.*

MAY 7, 1912.

Sighted St. Thomas's hills and Culebra.

Have a whole day's sail before us unless we get more wind.

Do those who marry in their teens find their duties of married life easier? I wouldn't be surprised if they do. I find my education getting in the way of giving in to my husband's selfish lust and blame myself for not being more amenable to the Julie O'Grady mentality. Kipling was off course when he said she and the Colonel's lady were sisters under the skin. That was male wishful thinking, ruddy Rudy, and rudely put.

Sunday morning. MAY 12, 1912.

Still not a whisper of a breeze but Fred enjoying the fishing. Caught several barracudas, and they're as tasty as they are ugly. Lowered the launch and towed the vessel several miles trying to make the entrance to Marinabo port. Anchored off Yabacao. The number of Portuguese names, ending in ao, assure me that many of the influential men in the Spanish discovery ships were Portuguese. Yet the Gallegos, from Galicia, speak Spanish with a heavy Portuguese influence. They can hardly be understood by the Andalusians, who mimic them.

Up sail and away this morning, but as Fred says so poetically, "This wind ain't a good fart."

Wrote to Mrs. Darrah, poor dear, and Myra and Betty and Father B. while Fred fretted and fished. Still almost calm, and I suppose many people would enjoy being here below the lovely hills of El Yunque, the anvil mountain, with its rain forest, but not if they had a cargo awaiting. I hate doldrums. Fred had target practice with his rifle when the big shark surfaced, got him, and shouted to him to go back and tell those who sent him that they'd get the same

treatment if they held the wind back any longer. I hope Neptune
won't be offended, or am I getting balmy, too?

MAY 17, 1912.

Anchored in the stream at Marinabo to load. Arrived Sunday and
shifted twice when soundings told us there was enough water nearer
land, where the little tugs with their barges won't have such a long
trip to make.

Lunched with Don Jorge at the finca Bordalaise and a most
attractive little spot it is. Jorge said he should not have let me marry
"El Godo." All Anglo-Saxons are to him what the Goths were to his
Iberian ancestors, who have transmitted down through the ages a
dislike for the crude barbarians who upset the Romano-Hispanic
civilization of the fifth century. That's a long memory! His brown
eyes and laissez-faire attitude may once have been charming to me,
but I thank God for devilish Fred, Maine, and all the other goodies
I'd have missed by being a Senora. Still, it's fun to be wooed when
you're thirty and pregnant. I told Miss H., and she was round-eyed
with Bostonian shock. How she'll do as a newspaper hen is beyond
me. But she does enjoy the *lechon asado*, the yucca, the plantains,
and the avacados, bless her little bean-fed tummy.

That was not nice, Dorothea. Miss H. has been very sweet and
helpful. Hasn't she been a joy helping with the embroidery on baby's
clothes! I do hope I haven't let her influence the design of the
clothes, though. All five slips could be spotted from afar as being of
Bostonian patterns, because they are so distressingly plain. From
my gay, Latin background, I've been tempted to add a few bright
colors and a curleque or two. How Don Jorge did compliment me on
the yellow shawl I wore with my blue gown for lunch at the finca.
Fred would have said I looked like an "old squaw," one of the gaily-
plumed seabirds he loves to shoot, the birds that must have been
named for the chattering and loud vocals of Penobscot Indian
women.

Miss H. hopes with me that this little baby will be good and
healthy and grow up to be straight and useful. If it's a boy, I want

him to be strong like his papa, manly and noble; if it's a little girl, please God make her dear and sweet and darling; and, oh how I do wish it would be one of each and that both live.

Dora, Dora, my girl, you must never, NEVER re-read or review what you have written. In that paragraph about the seabirds, you contumely condemned, by implication, your husband, whom you then proceeded to eulogize as the model for your baby. In one place you love him; in the other you hate him. But that may be realism, my dear. After all, aren't "old squaws" tasty? You'd better settle down, my dear, say in that little house at Herring Gut, where the long winter will poke some sense into you and deliver you from soaring from the heights of happiness to the depths of despair, all in one minute. Maine can be sobering.

And I do agree to having our own little home on land in delightful Port Clyde during these coming months, about four now, while I gather strength. Port Clyde is such a busy place I know I shan't be bored. It has ships visiting every day, and the factories provide action, and I shall steal a piece of land from Fred to start a town library, where the books I furnish can be read all winter by others as well as me so that we may discuss them. We'll get the blood of the Puritan descendants back on the intellectual route. Will it be possible? I know some of them want it. Will the fundamentalists cooperate or censor?

How many varieties of illnesses can a pregnant woman have? Or is it the diet aboard ship, the salt horse, salt mackerel, rock-hard biscuits, molasses cookies, and doughnuts without eggs. Yet I must be bright and pleasant for my husband's sake, even though my tummy feels like a rock, rolling rocks all bumping into each other.

MAY 29, 1912. (Puerto Rico, all around it and through it.)

It is many a long day, some dreary and some sparkling, since I have written in here. But today I must write for relief. Perhaps if I explode here I may be able to handle things more competently on this ship. Miss Henderson has sailed north with her impressions and her notes. God knows what the *Boston Herald* will print of us. Being typically Bostonian, she did not show her thoughts, and the newspaper write-up could be praiseworthy or condemnatory but, knowing her, I suppose it will be factual and not at all sensational. I do hope so. She spent three lovely days with us at Arroyo, on shore, and one day in Ponce and one as Miss Verge's guest, at Aguirre. There we went by auto for a delightful lunch with red-checked tablecloths just like Boston's waterfront restaurants, which made Miss H. feel she had never left home. We called on Mrs. Chisholm to get all the gossip. Miss Verge's brother came from Humacao to see us and had thousands of questions about his native Friendship and his brother Enos, the great sailor who navigates by the feel of the sea and wind. Miss Watts, she of the Thomaston tribe, spent a day and a night on board with us, a slight, dainty little lady like a pale, pink tearose, a fragile piece of Havilan china. Fred honors her great uncle, Captain Sam Watts, for whom a big square-rigger was named, but shies away from the little lady who would probably do a backwards somersault if Fred opened his mouth with his usual crudities. But I'm not fair; he can be so damned honey-tongued that it fairly sends me into gales of laughter, knowing what he is thinking while the goo oozes.

Yesterday I taught Spanish to several New England ladies who have just arrived for their husbands' stints at Aguirre. Also made fudge for Fred and Captains Rawding and Wallace, who were visiting us and spent the day sailing ships while moored to the land. Both of their vessels are waiting for the *Hopkins* to finish loading. We are four sailing vessels and one steamer at anchor here. When the trades don't blow, it is fun to wake in the morning as head ship of the anchored flotilla and, when the wind starts up, suddenly find we're the last ship in the fleet, all our ships turning with the wind or tide, which is slight. It's also fun to hear the false-dawn crowing of the roosters from land answering their brethren in the coops atop the houses of the anchored ships. No need for translators.

Tasted oysters plucked from the palm trees lining the channel; very good, and such a relief after the supper last night of salt beef and fried potatoes and a breakfast of cornmeal and salt mackerel, such a beautiful diet for a pregnant woman!

Oh, these easterners, especially those downeasters! Such selfish, niggardly tightwads. Fred refused to take me on shore for a decent meal, and then, while I ached so nothing but a backrub would console me, he snored! Had to massage myself and then damned if he didn't roll over in his sleep and grab me in those powerful arms to hold me. I couldn't move and finally had to knee him to get out of bed and seek some sleep in the hammock. I ought to have mutinied back in J-ville that first trip when he made me have the abortion and I may do it yet. And then the day before yesterday, when he lied to me. I knew he was equal to several different kinds of deviltry, but I did not know that he would lie to me directly. I asked him if he was going ashore and he said "no." Then, in a few moments, he took the launch and went, leaving me behind, and disappeared around the island looking for fish. Thank God it was only fish he was hunting. Then the devil returned with a grin and several letters to me, one from Miss Foote of J-ville. So exasperating. How I wish I were strong-minded enough to ignore that handsome grin and keep silent for a solid week, not talking to him at all. Then he would beg for conversation.

A good dinner on shore and afterwards, an awful pain. So many pains lately. I don't care about myself, my eating and my feelings, so much as I do care about the child. I must take care of myself. I shall see to it that I am properly treated. Fred has simply got to walk the chalk line or else.

Friday, JUNE 7, 1912.

Letters today. So Aunt Sue has known, ever since that awful episode in J-ville. [Editor's note: Aunt Sue Kingman, of the Brewster family, was a distant relative of Dorothea Moulton, with whom Dorothea stayed in Minneapolis while attending the University]. That awful Foote girl cannot keep her lips closed at all. But if Aunt Sue knew, why didn't she come on to Boston to see me? The Lord knows she has plenty of money, what with being chief heir to the Pillsbury monies. She writes that she has one of those new electric autos. I must get west to see her and take a ride.

Spent Wednesday and the night at Rio Blanco, Mr. Preston's country hacienda and finca. An eleven-course dinner! Wow, how Fred does manage to make up for the salt mackerel. Cool and pleasant in the heavy rains as we watched, while dining, from the veranda. And such a lovely big bed after our bunk. And no rolling of the ship. At first I missed the roll and could not sleep without it. My first evening on land since last September. Delicious grapefruit and how charmingly did our hosts act and talk. Wow! It made me cry, later, at what I've been missing, but, then, I guess pregnant women cry at almost anything. And think of what they have been missing. They may scintillate in their conversation, but who of them has walked barefoot in the rain forests of Tijuca or toured, incognito, the redlights of Rio. I finally understood Fred's unwillingness to talk. He has seen too much and knows too much for landlubbers. They would never understand. And I'm caught right in the middle. I love good conversation and yet I must be careful about talking of things I've seen. I don't want to be known as another Georges Sand, and Fred despises having people classify him *a la Munchausen*. So he confines his conversation to "Ayah," and "It might be," and "Yes, I was there," while I say, "Is that so?" and "Very interesting," which used in a Spanish conversation, *Muy interesante*, means "How dull." Seafarers are a distinct tribe, my girl, and now you're one, so take it for what it's worth and glory in its attributes. As Fred says about the old Greek fruit peddler who summed up life quite well with "What I make on the bananas, I lose on the potatoes," "You can't have it all." So, take the cash and let the credit go, my dear, as Omar said, nor heed the beatings of a distant drum. Damn the drums; I'll take ship's bells.

JUNE 17, 1912

Picnic on the island yesterday. I took the launch and by myself ferried the three American girls out for a swim. They were quite impressed with my boat-handling but I wasn't. Should not have beached her on that damned coral but on the beach of white sand in the little cove where we swam. One of them, Eva Boyden, will sail north with us. We picked up pink and white coral for souvenirs. Inside the reefs where I thought we'd all be safe from sharks and barracudas I swam face to face with a barracuda. First saw him staring at me about six feet ahead. I remembered what Fred had said about not making the slightest move. I froze. He stared. I stared back, under water and holding my breath. It seemed I would pop. He moved sidewise. I stayed still. When it seemed my lungs would burst or I would have a miscarriage from the pressure on my tummy, he sidled off seaward before I moved a muscle. What a relief to see the big-mouthed monster's tail. They can take a leg off as easily as swatting a fly, what with their inward slanted teeth. Of course I said nothing about it to the girls, but once on the beach I lay down for quite some time until my pulse rate fell below a thousand a minute. Whew!

Was to go uptown yesterday to see about that awful, baggy new dress, but guess I shall have to wait another day or so because the stevedores are enjoying a *huelga*, a strike, and that foolish man of mine is having all sorts of caniption fits and spasms.

Went to town after all and enjoyed it. May sail tomorrow. Visited Captain Sargent of the Bull Line steamer *Ruth*, named for one of the sugar-central wives. Had strawberries on board and enjoyed the clean and well-varnished cabin of the Captain. I wonder whether Mrs. Kent will like the steamer *Peter Crowell*, named for Captain Crowell, Mr. Thurlow's partner from Cape Cod. The lovely big and roomy cabin of the *Governor Powers* would suit me better than the tiny quarters, no matter how well varnished, of the *Ruth*. Captain Sargent says the *Peter Crowell* is not big enough for the Panama trade for which she was built; should be twice as large. I hope and believe he's wrong; Fred has put money in the *Crowell*, and she was built to go into ports where big steamers can't go when loaded deep. Would I prefer a steamer? The Captain's quarters are up so high. Ours are below and cool. They have refrigerators and cold storage, however, and quick trips compared to a schooner, but I do so love my little *Hopkins*. And it was in her that we did our courting and took our sea-going honeymoon and spent our first year of married life, to say nothing of our awful tragedy. Here we have been as happy as two, such as us, have a right to be.

JUNE 9, 1912. (At sea, homeward bound.)

Reading those parts of my diary that precede the Utuado entries, describing my indecision and decision to sail north as chaperone for Betty. I've plenty of time for once because Eva Boyden, with the constitution of an ox, makes the daily fudge, cleans the cabin, sews on baby's garments, bulldozes Fred, and is such a dear. What a holiday for little me! I've taught her to take the sights, and now she won't even compromise on the day's run with Fred but commands him to use her position instead of his and then comes to laugh and joke with me about how he stutters when she shows him where he added instead of subtracted. Dawsie is laughing, too, with me, of course, not with Fred, and Dawsie says we should sign Missy Boyden on forever. "She dat more of a skipper dan anyboady I see but my granny," says Dawsie.

From my 1908-1910 diaries, I know now that I was a vacuum in search of what I finally found. Imagine making entries about tea at Aunt Sue's and about cousin Harrison telling her of his petunias! And my decision to chuck the charity job Aunt Sue got for me and move on to the teaching job in Puerto Rico. Wasn't that wonderful? And I was so doubtful. Aunt Sue thought I was going to the ends of the earth; Mama cried and Papa threatened to take me back on the farm where the only men I'd have seen would have been Norwegian farmers who think they're funny calling alfalfa alfy-alphy. God preserved me. And the fat, stinking Sioux Indian squaws hogging the coach seats on the train run from Minneapolis to Dawson. And the insipidness of Chautauquas!

I wrote that I was glad to get east of Chicago, and I was. Niagara was a thrill to me then, but now it's a small waterfall compared to Brazil's enormous Iguasu. Back then I hadn't a clue that the "su" of Iguasu, just as the word Niagara, showed a connection with the

Altaic language of northern Asia, proof enough to me that the American Indians came from that area. Niagara is like the Turkish "ne akar," where there is water, and "su" as in Iguasu, Missouri, and other river names comes from the word for water, su, found also in Japanese. Teepee is from *tepe*, Turkish for tent. Allegheny means in that lingo the red hills. Eskimo is *eski*, Turkish for old, combined with *mo*, mongol.

Then when I sailed down the Hudson I did not know why I felt so good but now I know, from my Maine experience, that I felt like a salmon, an alewife, or a smelt, heading for my natural habitat, the open sea. New York was dirty, but I loved every one of its theaters and museums and I adore the Westminster hotel, which is French in patrons, English in waiters, and cheap in price. Saw the tipsy Flatiron building. Was shocked at land being worth $20,000 per square foot along Fifth Avenue, or so said the rubberneck bus announcer in his horrible Brooklyn accent. Passed Vanderbilt's white marble palace and two of Gould's, who couldn't stand not being more showy than the V.'s. The Astors, too, have a white marble home, while the Rockerfellers were inclined to the red for their Baptist church and had a gray stone house, to be different and show that they were not unchristianly gaudy. Riverside Drive, above impressive Grant's Tomb, was more tasteful. The roof of my hickish mouth must have gotten sunburned, back then, from gaping at the sights. And Tiffany's, lawsy-mercy, honey chile, how you did gawk! It must have been then that I decided that one day I would have a joyous array of candlesticks and Tiffany glass vases. And thanks to my wondrous Fred, I'm well on the way. We can afford some luxuries because Fred is such a successful shipmaster. While others hesitate, he acts. That's why the *Hopkins* pays dividends while other vessels require shareholders to pay "reverse" dividends to make up for the deficits and contribute toward keeping the vessel maintained and ready. If only Fred would go ashore and manage the fleet, they'd all pay like the *Hopkins*. But he won't, he loves too much to sail her. And that's certainly all right with me. So long as he entrusts the management to smart old Mr. Thurlow, we'll be all right, especially with Fred putting money into steamers.

My diary tells me that while in New York I saw John Mason at little white Hacketts in the *Witching Hour*. It seems aeons ago. After the Metropolitan Museum enchanted me with the Corots, Turners, and Borghums, I finally looked at my watch and had to rush back to the hotel, grab my suitcase, catch the subway on the run, and get to the *SS Coamo*, bound for Puerto Rico, just as they were taking in the gangway. There's a note in my log that I sighed with relief at leaving, but I must get back to little old New York again, now that I have the beginnings of appreciation.

Eighty U.S. teachers on board bound down to teach the Puerto Ricans English. Weren't we fools to think we could make them over into our own images! And wasn't the Department of the Interior misguided to try it! What a shame it would have been had we been successful. That wonderful culture destroyed. Shades of the Penobscot Indians!

Apparently I discovered Puerto Rico on September 23, 1908, just a few centuries after Ponce de Leon and was ordered to his namesake, Ponce, for assignment. The last night on board the *Coamo* we all gathered aft following our baked-bean supper and the ship's music, and we sang into the night until, after a short sleep in deck chairs, we sighted Morro Castle and steamed in past an Argentine ship, which had been quarantined for months with yellow jack. Little did I know about such things. Was impressed by the oxcarts along the road to Ponce, the narrow streets, the lack of yards in front of the houses, and the pastel greens, blues, oranges, pinks, and yellows of the houses, things I hardly notice now. At Ponce went to the Hotel Inglaterra where was met by Mr. Terry, the school superintendent, a fine man from Boston. He told me that breakfast for Puerto Ricans was only *cafe con leche,* but that the waiters, knowing I was *una gringa* would serve me with fruit and an egg. Imagine being so naive that it showed on my face, or was he telling that to all the girls? How I was impressed with the Spanish wooing and the red uniform of the *bomberos,* the firemen, of Ponce. Oh, to live that innocent series of surprises once again! And milking the cows into a bottle. Then boiling it. I'd never heard of such things. And the way you learned Spanish so quickly, not out of a crashing intellectual effort, I'm sorry to say, but out of a devilish ability at mimicry. Oh it was a heavenly two years, but am I ever glad Freddy-boy happened by. I shall have to do more often this research into my past but not now. New England and childbirth are coming up on the horizon, and I must start my packing.

DECEMBER 11, 1912. (At home in Herring Gut, known to the better element as Port Clyde.)

Eva Boyden came with us to Maine, and she was such a rock to lean on through all the trials we've had since that entry I made when sailing away from Puerto Rico. There's been so much to write about but no time to write. Now as I get well from my long siege there's finally time, and, as Doctor North forbids me any activity, I can find time to read and write by the fireplace, which I love and over which there is a large and lovely painting of my *Hopkins.*

Captain J.W. was shot on board his schooner while at Martinique. He died there, and the body was shipped home for burial on the Ridge. From what I gather he and the ship's engineer, one Cook who Fred said was never any good and who, Fred said, should have been strangled at the time Fred had his hands on Cook's throat, went ashore to deliver some revolvers requested by a local Frenchman from a past trip. The Frenchman refused the guns. Captain Will went back to the ship, but the engineer went to a rum shop. When he returned on board he was crazed and went aft to where Captain J.W. was sleeping in his hammock and shot him. Captain Will's last words, heard by the mate and several crew members, were, "Everything goes to Fred." My poor boy is now saddled with not only going out to Martinique at the Consul's request for the trial of Cook, but he also has to tend the local Balano interests, the water company, the tenements, the wood business, and the sale of the Wawendnock to the Harrises, who have never paid all the bills regarding the purchase of that lovely place which should never have been sold. I'd love to live there.

I was confined for weeks at Knox Hospital, my baby boy having been the first baby born there. James Wilfred, named for his grandfather who would have loved him but whom he will never see, is a dear, precious little darling son, born on September 2, his father's birthday. He's now just over three months and had to be put on a bottle, poor little chap, because his mother didn't take care of herself on her rovings and drink enough milk with the salt mackerel.

Was just interrupted by Isaiah Balano, delivering the wood for my winter fireplace fire. He also dumped off a load for the schoolhouse and the roar woke Wilfred. I told Isaiah about his brother's death and let him read Fred's letter from Martinique. The jurymen of the murder were twelve French-speaking blacks. Fred is going from Martinique down to Barbados and thence home on the mail steamer to New York. I wrote to find out his arrival date and shall go to New York to meet him no matter what Doctor North says against my trip. The poor boy needs me now more than ever. And just to think that a year ago we were so happily entering lovely Rio. And I was hurt because Fred was giving me a gangway instead of a baby. Now I have both, however, and can't wait to see Wilfred creeping up the gangway, bound for Rio, all three of us.

Friday, DECEMBER 13, 1912.

I told Dr. North, a wonderful physician, to go back to Bowdoin College and study some psychology in order to learn that the best cure for a woman is to go and meet her husband. He laughed and said he guessed Captain Fred could find his way home without my navigation. So I read *Daddy Longlegs* by the lovely fire, about a girl who wrote letters to a man she didn't know but later married. Very bright but quite dangerous for her.

A letter from Puerto Rico tells me that my good old friend, Mr. Benedict of Hatillo, has passed away, leaving a pregnant widow who has gone to her brother's in Mississippi. Little Bernard has been shipped off to his sister, Mabel, my old teaching comrade at Utuado, who now lives in Oneanta, N.Y., and whom I shall visit if I can make the trip to meet Fred at the dock in New York City. But Dr. North says my convalescence still needs inactivity for a month of Sundays. No news from the *Hopkins*, temporarily commanded by another, or from Fred or from the Royal Mail about the ship on which Fred is supposed to arrive from Barbados. I'd convalesce faster if Jim Wilson and his rushing horses would get me something in the mail instead of magazines, advertisements, and bills. Why doesn't Fred telegraph me? Why doesn't he take the French steamer from Fort-de-France? Has he the typically English and American distaste and distrust of French ships? I'd love wine with my meals and a dish of bouillabaisse before my filet mignon and crepes suzettes to top it off, with a bit of Camembert to boot. It would be a welcome and far cry from Mother B's menu of cold porridge for breakfast, stale ham for lunch, and crackers with milk, sour milk at that, for supper. Her penny-pinching affects my health also, with the lack of heat. Captain J.W. installed a hot-water system for heating, radiators and a new coal-burning furnace, but she won't use it because the price of coal is greater than the cost of cutting wood from her own woodlots. That would be reasonable, I suppose, if she allowed the cutters to cut more than what is needed for her kitchen stove and a bit for the fireplace, but she doesn't. The radiators must be frozen because there's no heat in the upstairs bedrooms. To keep from freezing, I must nap by the fireplace. Although some days she's not so vexing as usual, I do wait for Fred to straighten her out. Childbirth was not the cure-all for me that she claims it was for her (why did she have just the one child?), and I am in pain so often that I can't fight, especially in her own home.

To escape for a short while, I attended the Sewing Circle at the Advent Church and tonight will go to the annual sale at Mrs. Marshall's Bazaar. Shall have the Tibbetts girl in to care for Wilfred. She is so attentive and sweet with him and would never let him come to any harm.

At Mrs. Marshall's, I bought little Dutch bonnets made by Lena Harris. They are so fetching and make lovely presents. The center part is blue and pink muslin with white embroidery in matching colors. I shall send one to Eva Boyden, who is spending the year at

Fajardo in a splendid position as principal. Awfully glad for the wondrous girl. Must get baby's photos from Rockland. Must get together a group interested in having a village library. There's so much to do that I shouldn't let Mother B. bother me. How I do miss Fred, who has been twice as gentle to me since his father died, not nearly so cross. It will be five weeks tomorrow that the poor boy has been gone on his fruitless errand. The jury acquitted the murderer, and the Consul wrote me privately that he believes it was due to the blacks being so scared of white Frenchmen having guns. They ignored the murder and ganged up against gun-running. I do find some sympathy with them, I must admit, and wasn't it a shame that Captain J.W. should get involved in such foolishness, but, as the Consul wrote, every skipper visiting Martinique is requested to bring in guns. The situation, he says, is such that the whites, a tiny minority, feel threatened every hour of the day and night and must protect themselves or flee their island.

I got word of Fred's arrival date and telegraphed cousin Roscoe to meet him. Shall try to get shiftless Roy Hupper, he who mismanages the water works, to drive me in the machine to Thomaston when Fred's train arrives.

DECEMBER 16, 1912.

Hurrah! Hurrah! Came a telegram this morning from Fred. He arrived in New York and is coming home at once. I am so glad. He'll get the furnace going and rub my back and play with his little son. Wilfred laughed so coyly at me when I told him his Daddy was coming home. You'd think he almost understood. He is a perfect dear and more fun than a basket of monkeys.

DECEMBER 17, 1912.

Fred came home on the SS Monhegan today. I had made fudge and stuffed dates for him. I had also decorated our room and embroidered pillows for his homecoming. I should have known better. All the thanks I got was, "Where in hell have you hidden Nellie's pillow?" Also. I purposely gave up an invitation to meet with my library group because Fred was coming home, and damned if he didn't go out and spend the whole evening with nasty Perce Hupper, his bastard cousin. I do get so everlastingly weary of being the only one to do the square thing. And how my poor back does ache from doing all those things for his arrival. I'd better get him away from his mother soon. Shall we go to sea in the *Hopkins* or in Father J.W.'s *Margaret Thomas?* I don't care, just so long as we go.

DECEMBER 22, 1912.

Uptown to Rockland today after the bad storm yesterday. Had to go on the mail carriage with Jim Wilson's racing horses, because the snow was too deep for the Regal to manage. We got stuck three times before we got out of the village. Bought Christmas cards and many goodies at Fuller, Cobbs. Tried condensed milk for Wilfred, so he can get used to it before going on shipboard. Used some this evening instead of sending young Alton up to Leonard Seavey's for fresh milk [Editor's note: Leonard Seavey lived up Horse Point Road, in the house later taken over by N.C. Wyeth, where Andrew Wyeth spent his summers].

Have received many packages from friends but shall not open them until Christmas morning. Sent sister Nettie a bracelet from Rio and sister Myra a check for $25 to help out at the University. Must thank Fred for being able to do so much more than I ever used to be able to do about giving presents. Much of what I wrote about his stinginess in the first part of these diaries should be deleted. He has a native generosity which, sometimes, allows him to overcome his mother's training toward making every penny holler for mercy.

DECEMBER 23, 1912.

Took Granma Balano her Christmas presents, baby's photo, and a white woolen vest. Mailed cousin Marjorie's and Aunt Mary's

presents, also from Rio; also went into the woods and selected
Wilfred's Christmas tree, baked Indian pudding, and trotted down
cellar for raspberry sauce to top it with. Did a thousand things to
keep busy. Wilfred seems to thrive on condensed milk, and that
makes me happy because he will soon go to sea where that is all we
can supply him with.

Now Mr. Diary, here's a proposition for you, or a riddle to
solve. It is about living with Fred's mother. Fred never did stay at
home evenings and never will. He is the prima donna in that lowlife
Perce's store, glorying in being admired by the lobstermen, the
factory workers, and the coastal sailors. How do I manage to move
into the little house across from the chapel right away, so that when
we return from our trips at sea I shall have my own home? Fred
merely sleeps at his mother's and can't stand being there during
waking hours. Do I tell him that I can't stand it, either? He should
understand, but will he? I doubt it. But if I were to spend my
evenings out, as he does, where would I go? I certainly don't want to
listen to the women's gossip every evening. And I don't dare talk to
anyone here of anything besides who is sleeping with whom. Shall I
just walk out and startle him? Think it over, diary, and I'll be waiting.

JANUARY 2, 1913

Son Billy is four months old today and a dear little fellow, too.
He has sported short clothes since his Daddy got the furnace going
and weighs 15 pounds. His foolish mama wheeled him all the way
over to Watson Balano's today to see his greatgrandmother and
resultamente his mama has a furious backache.

Letters from Myra and Aunt Sue. Heard today that the *SS
Savannah* was lost on Frying Pan Shoals, and Captain Giles's
schooner was lost off Sandy Hook. I became a member of the
Eastern Star, although I don't want to be a "joiner." The Masonic
order is very strong in St. George what with so many descendants of
Scots and Scotch-Irish protestants. The members see to it that their

lodge brothers are selectmen and tax assessors and sheriffs. Woebetide a catholic who enters here, although he'd never know what he was up against until it hit him. Huey Dunn, he of legend, was a catholic. 'Tis said of him that he jumped overboard in Halifax harbor, escaping with a fellow Irishman from a British frigate, back in the seventies. In the icy waters, Huey said he was cold and his mate told him to turn up his coat collar. He wore it ever afterwards turned up, but he changed his religion soon after finding out that he couldn't get a job in any of the local factories. After that he prospered.

After Fred's bout with Mother B. about the price of coal, he now talks of building a coal shed on the shore and dealing in coal. However, it seems as if that dream is on the level with buying a farm out west, because when a report came today that the *Hopkins* had been reported off Montauk, Fred told me to get ready to leave with him to join her. Am worried about Billy getting along on condensed milk, but I must go and take him with me. The lamp has gone out here in this gloomy, gloomy house, and I want no more of this sadness. As Dawsie would say, "I done got de miseries." And Fred just won't stay at home. Once away at sea I shall recover quickly, I know, and Billy will be alright. I shall consult every doctor at Harvard about getting the right formula for his health. Then, when we return to Herring Gut, I shall have my own place, and, as Fred said en route to Rio, it will have a fireplace, a good bath, a furnace, and something he didn't add, a full library.

JANUARY 6, 1913.

At sea, glory be, and it's Three King's Day, too.

What a wonderful present from The Three Kings, *Los Tres Reyes Magicos*. We are loaded to the gunwales with a full cargo for enchanting England. I wonder, did Mr. and Mrs. Lykes have anything to do with this? Maybe, because we have scores of long masts as deck load. On deck last night, my diamond sparkled in the starlight and so did I, Fred said. Our baby turned in his little hammock and sighed. The nanny goat recommended by the Harvard professors blatted a protest about being milked by the old steward for Billy's midnight milk, and the little kitten Fred got for Billy came purring at my feet for protection against the cold, which I don't feel because I am all warm inside. I am speaking Spanish as well as English to our son and, for myself, learning French. We shall do England before crossing over to Bordeaux to load wine for Boston. Selah!